40 days

WITH THE CELTIC SAINTS

D0543570

The Bible Reading Fellowship
15 The Chambers, Vineyard
Abingdon OX14 3FE
brf.org.uk

The Bible Reading Fellowship (BRF) is a Registered Charity (233280)

ISBN 978 0 85746 548 1
First published 2017
10 9 8 7 6 5 4 3 2 1 0
All rights reserved

Text © David Cole 2017
The author asserts the moral right to be identified as the author of this work

Cover image © Marcin Dobas / Alamy

Acknowledgements
Unless otherwise stated, scripture quotations are taken from the World English Bible
(public domain)

Scripture quotations taken from The Holy Bible, New International Version (Anglicised
edition) copyright © 1979, 1984, 2011 by Biblica. Used by permission of Hodder & Stoughton
Publishers, a Hachette UK company. All rights reserved. 'NIV' is a registered trademark of Biblica.
UK trademark number 1448790

Scripture quotations taken from the Holy Bible, New Living Translation, copyright © 1996, 2004,
2007, 2013. Used by permission of Tyndale House Publishers, Inc., Carol Stream, Illinois 60188.
All rights reserved

Scripture taken from *THE MESSAGE*. Copyright © 1993, 1994, 1995, 1996, 2000, 2001, 2002.
Used by permission of NavPress Publishing Group

Extract from 'The Dream of the Rood' in *The Anglo-Saxon World*.
Reproduced by permission of The Agency (London) Ltd
© Kevin Crossley-Holland, 1981
First published by The Boydell Press
All rights reserved and enquiries to The Agency (London) Ltd
24 Pottery Lane, London W11 4LZ fax: 0207 727 9037

Every effort has been made to trace and contact copyright owners for material used in this
resource. We apologise for any inadvertent omissions or errors, and would ask those concerned
to contact us so that full acknowledgement can be made in the future

A catalogue record for this book is available from the British Library

Printed and bound by CPI Group (UK) Ltd, Croydon CR0 4YY

40 DAYS
with the
CELTIC
SAINTS

DEVOTIONAL READINGS
FOR A TIME OF PREPARATION

DAVID COLE

Contents

Introduction

'Celtic' is a term which has become quite common in modern parlance, and can often be, as J.R.R. Tolkien once said, 'a magic bag, into which anything may be put, and out of which almost anything may come'.[1] When speaking historically it usually refers to the people groups who inhabited Britain, Ireland and north-west France before and during the time of the Roman military occupation. The Celts were a community- or clan-based society who were rural and close to nature and the rhythms of the land. In *The Gallic Wars*, written in the first century BC, Julius Caesar states, 'The whole of Gaul is divided into three parts; of these one is inhabited by the Belgae, a second by the Aquitani, and the third by a people called *Celts* in their own language and Gauls in ours.'[2] The term, however, does not seem to have been used much during or immediately following the Roman occupation; it is never mentioned by Bede, for example, in any of his writings. Although it can be slightly ambiguous to readers today, it is also a helpful term, as Oliver Davies explains in *Celtic Spirituality*:

> 'Celtic', though potentially misleading, remains a useful term in its inclusivity, and is generally to be preferred to 'Irish', 'Welsh', or even 'insular', which—though entirely appropriate in many contexts—are too exclusivist… [The use of the term 'Celtic'] does maintain the principle of an affinity of language, supporting some kind of affinity of culture between the Celtic-speaking areas, reinforced by extensive cultural contact based on close geographical proximity.[3]

So the term 'Celtic' can be useful today to help identify a certain collection of peoples and tribes and kin. Even though there may have been differences in their specifics, there are enough similarities to enable us to see a connection—which, if true for the people, would also follow when speaking of the 'Celtic' church. Although there were, historically, differences between the Irish, Pictish and Brittonic churches, again there are enough similarities to enable us to see a connection. As Thomas O'Loughlin states in *Celtic Theology*:

> In Ireland itself, Archbishop James Ussher (1581–1656) was gathering and publishing other materials. His *Britannicarum Ecclesiarum Antiquitates* of 1639, while not using the words 'Celtic Church', can be seen as putting the concept into circulation that in the early medieval period there were distinct churches in these islands, distinct from one another and from Rome.[4]

When it comes to Celtic Christianity, we are speaking of a distinct style and expression of the Christian faith which reflected the life and community of these 'Celtic' people groups. Being close to nature and the rhythms of the land, they were also close to the Spirit of God within the surrounding creation, with little or sometimes no influence from the church and hierarchy that was growing out of the old Roman empire.

For the Celtic Christians of the first millennium AD, there were specific times in the year when they would spend 40 days in spiritual preparation. This time of preparation, or 'Lent', was implemented not only before the Easter celebrations but also before the Christmas ones. The 'Lesser Lent' of the Celtic Advent was observed in a similar fashion, not only as a time of preparation for the celebrations of the first coming of Christ, the incarnation, but also as a time to contemplate the second coming of Christ, ensuring that they were prepared for that too. Celtic Advent, or the Lesser Lent, began on the evening of 15 November, 40 days before 25 December (including Sundays).

However, these were not the only times at which the Celtic saints set aside a period of 40 days in preparation. Before Brendan set out on his most famous voyage, for example, he spent a 40-day period in prayer and fasting (see Chapter 6 for more details).

The concept of the number 40 representing a time of preparation is reflected in Jewish stories and practices, such as the account of Jesus going into the desert for 40 days before he began his ministry. It would have been a normal mindset for a Jew to think of 40 days of preparation before a major new beginning—hence our 40-day Lent and the ancient Celtic 40-day Advent, following the Jewish example.

So this book, *40 Days with the Celtic Saints*, can be used in your preparations and as an aid to meditation for the 40 days leading up to Easter, as we would understand Lent to be, but it can also be used for the 40-day Lesser Lent, or Celtic Advent. Alternatively, following the Jewish and Celtic Christian understanding, it could be used as a 40-day preparation for any significant event, or as a general 40-day consecutive meditation, with no special event at the end.

You could also come back to the book throughout the year, reading about each saint on their feast day (the day they were 'born into glory', as the Celtic Christians would say—the day their earthly bodies stopped and their soul was transferred to the spiritual realm/heaven). The saints are presented in alphabetical order, but a list in the order of their feast days is included at the back of the book.

Lent is a significant part of the modern church calendar. It helps us to prepare for the important celebration of Easter. Lent begins 40 days (plus Sundays) before Easter Day, on the evening of Shrove Tuesday/ morning of Ash Wednesday, and is meant to be a time for us to gain an understanding, through giving something up, of what it means to sacrifice. Then, by the time we get to the Easter weekend and contemplate the death of Christ on the cross, we can comprehend, to a small degree, what it meant for Jesus to give up his life.

Each of the following 40 readings offers a short biography of a Celtic saint, some scripture, a prayer and a meditation. Some of the biographies are longer than others as much more is known about some saints than about others. None of them is less important than any other, however; it is simply that different amounts were written down about them. We know, for example, a great deal about the saints who had influence within the Northumbrian kingdom and much of what is now England, as Bede wrote extensively about them, but he did not write much about the saints in Wales. Ireland has some good histories on certain saints, but other information has been lost. Much of the information was lost during raids and invasions, such as (but not only) at the time of the Vikings.

I hope the following 40 readings will be an inspiration for you, drawing you into a closer and more intimate relationship with God. I hope they deepen both your understanding and your heart, and I hope that the lives of the saints recorded here will cause you to want to become more Christ-like in the actions you take every day.

Using this book during one of the Lent periods

Lent before Easter

Over the 40 days leading up to Easter, the Celts remembered the suffering and victory of Christ and the work of the cross. The main teaching of the cross of Christ for the Celts was the *Christus Victor* concept, based on verses such as 1 John 3:8, which says, 'To this end the Son of God was revealed: that he might destroy the works of the devil', and Colossians 2:15, which says, 'Having stripped the principalities and the powers, he made a show of them openly, triumphing over them [on the cross].' This is quite different from today's Western Church emphasis on the concept of substitution.[5] A great example of the main teaching on the cross of Christ can be found in the Anglo-Saxon poem *The Dream of the Rood*. This poem depicts a Christ quite different from the one you are probably used to, in our Western churches.

Although the fullest recording of *The Dream of the Rood* is from the tenth-century Vercelli text, there is evidence to suggest that the poem was part of the Christian tradition long before that. One of these pieces of evidence is the Ruthwell Cross, from the heart of the Celtic Christian lands in northern Britain. The Ruthwell Cross has lines of *The Dream of the Rood* engraved upon it, and is commonly believed to have been carved in the late seventh century, between the Synod of Whitby and the time of Bede. As words from the poem form part of the cross, the poem would have been included in the Christian oral tradition for some time before that.

To begin your preparation for the Lent of Easter from a Celtic perspective, here are a few lines from *The Dream of the Rood*:

Listen! I will describe the best of dreams which I dreamed in the middle of the night when, far and wide, all men slept.

It seemed to me I saw a wondrous tree soaring into the air, surrounded by light, the brightest of crosses; that emblem was entirely cased in gold; beautiful jewels were strewn around its foot…

I saw the glorious tree joyfully gleaming, adorned with garments, decked in gold; the tree of the Ruler was rightly adorned with rich stones; yet through that gold I could see the agony once suffered by wretches, for it bled… I saw that sign often change its clothing and hue, at times dewy with moisture, stained by flowing blood, at times adorned with treasure…

[Then] I heard it utter words; the finest of trees began to speak: 'I remember the morning a long time ago that I was felled… men shifted me on their shoulders and set me on a hill…

I saw the Lord of Mankind hasten with such courage to climb upon me… the young warrior, God Almighty, stripped himself, firm and unflinching. He climbed upon the cross, brave before many, to redeem mankind. I quivered when the hero clasped me… A rood was I raised up; I bore aloft the mighty King, the Lord of Heaven… They drove dark nails into me… I was drenched in the blood that streamed from the Man's side after He set His spirit free…

They took Almighty God away. The warrior left me standing there, stained with blood… They laid Him down, limb-weary; they stood at the [warrior's] head, they beheld there the Lord of Heaven; and there He rested for a while, worn-out after batle. And then they began to build a sepulchre.'[6]

Lent before Christmas

The Celtic Christians believed that the incarnation of Christ was not just shown through Mary in the physical birth of Jesus, but that it is happening all the time through the birth of Jesus spiritually within us—not just once at 'conversion', but repeatedly, each time we make the choice to walk in the ways of Christ rather than walk our own way.

Preparation throughout the Lesser Lent also means ensuring that we are ready not only to welcome Christ within ourselves, but also to welcome him when he returns to reconcile all things to God at the end of the age. Over the 40 days leading up to Christmas, the Celts remembered the three comings of Christ:

- The coming of Christ in physical form as a baby through Mary.
- The coming of Christ into our lives in Spirit, through our faith.
- The coming of Christ at the end of the age to reconcile all things to God.

As part of your Lesser Lent preparation for Christmas from a Celtic perspective, contemplate the three comings of Christ within your own context and life.

May your time of Advent be one of preparation for the coming of Christ, not just a consumer-driven rush of partying and purchasing.

Whether at Christmas or at Easter, the Celtic Christians, reflecting the culture they came from, threw great feasts for the celebration days. Don't forget that Lent is about the preparation. Make sure you have the celebration as well!

The

40

Saints

I

Adamnan

FEAST DAY: 23 September (d.704)

Adamnan (sometimes Adomnan) was born around 30 years after the death of his relative Columba, and in 679 he became abbot of Iona. He was 'a good and wise man with an excellent knowledge of the scriptures'.[7] Adamnan is the author of the best-known *Life* of Columba, from which we get a great deal of knowledge of the early Irish-based Celtic Christian beliefs, but he wrote other things too. On meeting Arculf, a bishop of Gaul who had travelled extensively throughout the holy lands, Adamnan wrote down all that he heard from him and created a book, *De Locis Sanctis (On the Holy Places)*, so that the common folk would be able to get an idea of what the lands of Christ were really like, as many of them could not travel there. For two whole chapters of *The Ecclesiastical History of the English People* Bede paraphrases sections from the book,[8] and these words of Bede are now all that remain of Adamnan's *De Locis Sanctis*.

Adamnan also went on mission from Iona to the Anglian kingdom of Northumbria, where he met King Aldfrith and negotiated the release of 60 Irish hostages.[9] While he was there, Adamnan was immersed in the Romanised style of Christianity which had been implemented in all English monasteries after the Synod of Whitby in 664. The adoption of the Roman style included a different way of calculating the date of Easter, which had been quite contentious. Adamnan was a man who 'greatly loved unity and peace'[10] and so, on his return to Iona, he tried to implement the agreed Roman dating of Easter, but was met with great opposition. He travelled to Ireland, where too he introduced the new dating, and numerous places there accepted and adopted it. Travelling back to Iona, after celebrating Easter in Ireland, he tried for the next few months to get the monastery to accept the Romanised dating, but they still refused. That autumn Adamnan died, 'so that he was not compelled, when Eastertime returned, to have a still graver controversy with those who would not follow him in [the dating of Easter]'.[11]

Meditation

Spend a few moments simply resting. Breathe gently and slowly. Become aware of the constant presence of God which envelops you and permeates you.

Adamnan was a man who desired others to grow in their knowledge of the holy, writing about the lives of other saints and about the holy lands, so that those who could not get there might know something of them. He was also a man who desired unity and peace, and so he did his utmost to try to help create one universal church.

How might you inspire others to know more of the holiness of God and the unity of the church?

Spend time with God now, dwelling upon this question.

Scripture

Not for these only do I pray, but for those also who believe in me through their word, that they may all be one; even as you, Father, are in me, and I in you, that they also may be one in us; that the world may believe that you sent me. The glory which you have given me, I have given to them; that they may be one, even as we are one; I in them, and you in me, that they may be perfected into one; that the world may know that you sent me, and loved them, even as you loved me.'

JOHN 17:20–23

Blessing

May the inspiration of the Celtic saints draw you more closely into the heart of God.

May you be an inspiration to those around you who walk the faith with you.

May you be one who embodies unity in the body of Christ, without the need for uniformity, making others like ourselves.

2

Æbbe

FEAST DAY: 25 August (d.683)

Æbbe (pronounced 'Eeb') was the sister of Oswald, Oswin and Oswiu, all kings of Northumbria. During the kingdom wars within Northumbria and with Mercia, when she and her brothers were children, they were all sent by King Edwin, then king of Northumbria, to Iona for safety, where they were taught the Columban way of Christianity.

At some time in the mid-seventh century, Æbbe became abbess of the 'monastery of virgins' at Coldingham, which Cuthbert visited. The end of Coldingham monastery came through a devastating fire, and although it was said that the fire was caused by carelessness, 'all who knew the truth were easily able to judge that it happened because of the wickedness of those who dwelt there and especially of those who were supposed to be its leaders'.[12]

One of the monks at Coldingham, Adamnan (not Adamnan of Iona), 'who led a life so devoted to God in austerity and prayer… [and] often spent whole nights in vigils and prayers',[13] had a prophetic vision of the monastery burning as he returned from a journey. As soon as he went back into the monastery, Æbbe was informed of his vision. It was seen as a warning from God of the coming destruction of the monastery, in the same manner as the warning given to Nineveh in the time of Jonah.

The problem was that no one in the monastery, other than Adamnan and Æbbe, was interested in repenting of their godless lifestyle. They would 'remain awake for the purpose of sin. And the cells that were built for praying and for reading have become haunts of feasting, drinking, gossip, and other delights; even the virgins who are dedicated to God put aside all respect for their profession and… adorn themselves… to make friends with strange men.'[14]

Because Æbbe was a holy and devout woman, God did not allow the destruction to happen until after her death.

Meditation

Spend a few moments simply resting. Breathe gently and slowly. Become aware of the constant presence of God which envelops you and permeates you.

Æbbe was a devout and holy woman who led a community of God. She was humbly willing to admit and repent of her failings when a fellow believer gently pointed them out, while all others around her stubbornly refused.

How willing are you to admit and repent of your failings? Are you the kind of person who will stubbornly put up defences, or are you willing to listen humbly to gentle reproach?

Spend time with God now, dwelling upon these questions.

Scripture

Therefore let us also, seeing we are surrounded by so great a cloud of witnesses, lay aside every weight and the sin which so easily entangles us, and let us run with patience the race that is set before us, looking to Jesus, the author and perfecter of faith, who for the joy that was set before him endured the cross, despising its shame, and has sat down at the right hand of the throne of God.

HEBREWS 12:1–2

Blessing

May you know the loving guidance of God drawing you on in him.
May you be willing to hear the reproach of others if your life is not in
    line with the will of God.
May you know the leading of God in repentance and forgiveness,
    so that you can become more and more like him.

3
Aidan

FEAST DAY: 31 August (d.651)

Aidan came from Iona to lead a mission to the kingdom of Northumbria after the failure of a previous mission.

King Oswald had inherited the throne, but, having been sent to Iona as a child during the kingdom wars, he wanted his new people, the Angles of Northumbria, to gain a proper knowledge of Christianity. They had fallen away from the faith when the Christian King Edwin had been killed in 633. The monks who led the first mission went back to Iona reporting that the Angles were 'intractable, obstinate, and uncivilised'. Aidan suggested that perhaps these monks had been too harsh on the Angles and that they needed 'the milk of simpler teaching, as the apostle recommends, until little by little, as they grew strong on the food of God's word, they were capable of receiving more elaborate instructions'.[15]

At this suggestion, the gathering of monks agreed that Aidan should be consecrated as bishop and sent to Northumbria to see if his approach would work. Aidan therefore brought a small group of monks from Iona and established his monastic centre on Lindisfarne, the first Christian centre on that island.

Aidan walked the kingdom, sharing the gospel with those he met. He walked, rather than riding a horse, so that he could engage with the people without seeming to be above them, either physically or in status. He spent time in the slave markets, using money that had been given for the work in the monastery, to buy slaves. Once he had bought them, he would allow them to choose freedom or a place of learning in his monastery. Many chose the place of learning, and so began one of the first schools for the English (Angles) in history.

Aidan exhibited great spiritual power, mixed with a gentle love and humility. He performed wonderful miracles, including driving a great fire away from the gates of Bamburgh Castle, through prayer, when the pagan King Penda attacked. He showed great acts of humility and grace: for example, on one occasion when the king had commanded him to ride, he gave away the horse, with its royal trappings, to a beggar on the side of the road. He was also a man truly loved by others, even those who opposed his theology. Bede tells us that numerous monks and bishops from the church of Rome took council with Aidan, and that the difference between the two streams of church (the Celtic and the Roman), regarding the date of Easter, was tolerated while Aidan was alive 'because they had clearly understood that although he could not keep Easter otherwise than according to the manner of those who sent him, he nevertheless laboured diligently to practise the works of faith, piety and love, which is the mark of all the saints'.[16]

This tolerance, based on the respect that the Roman church had for Aidan personally, does not seem to have been granted to the Celtic church leaders after Aidan's death. Perhaps this contributed to the calling of the Synod of Whitby in 664.

Bede described Aidan thus:

> A man of outstanding gentleness, devotion and moderation who had a zeal for God... Such were his love of peace and charity, temperance and humility; his soul which triumphed over anger and greed and at the same time despised pride and vainglory... he made it his business to omit none of the commands of the evangelists, the apostles, and the prophets... and the best recommendation of his teaching to all was that he taught no other way of life than that which he himself practised.[17]

He wasn't so much someone who practised what he preached as someone who only preached what he practised.

Aidan was a pioneer with a great heart and an amazing strength of character. He shared the gospel with a foreign people (with King Oswald's help in translating from Aidan's Irish Gaelic to the language of the Angles). He was a man of 'outstanding gentleness, devotion and moderation who had a zeal for God'.

Meditation

Spend a few moments simply resting. Breathe gently and slowly. Become aware of the constant presence of God which envelops you and permeates you.

Aidan was a man who had humble beginnings, and, despite his rise, he remained humble throughout. He influenced mighty rulers and lowly slaves; he saw all people as equal in the eyes of God and therefore treated them all as equal, regardless of their earthly status.

How do you treat different people? Do you distinguish one person or people group from another, as better or more deserving? How might you become better at treating everyone as equal and humbly seeing them as one with God?

Spend time with God now, dwelling upon these questions.

Scripture

My brothers, don't hold the faith of our Lord Jesus Christ of glory with partiality. For if a man with a gold ring, in fine clothing, comes into your synagogue, and a poor man in filthy clothing also comes in; and you pay special attention to him who wears the fine clothing, and say, 'Sit here in a good place'; and you tell the poor man, 'Stand there,' or 'Sit by my footstool'; haven't you shown partiality among yourselves, and become judges with evil thoughts? Listen, my beloved brothers. Didn't God choose those who are poor in this world to be rich in faith, and heirs of the Kingdom which he promised to those who love him? But you have dishonoured the poor man. Don't the rich oppress you, and personally drag you before the courts? Don't they blaspheme the honourable name by which you are called? However, if you fulfil the royal law, according to the Scripture, 'You shall love your neighbour as yourself,' you do well. But if you show partiality, you commit sin, being convicted by the law as transgressors.

JAMES 2:1–9

Blessing

May you understand the great spiritual power which dwells within you.
May you treat everyone you meet equally without partiality.
May you only instruct others in those things that you already embody.

4
Bede

FEAST DAY: 25 May (d.735)

Bede is best known as a writer and historian, most famously for writing *The Ecclesiastical History of the English People* by royal decree. The book was completed in 731, and from it we get a huge amount of knowledge about Insular (Celtic) Christianity from the fifth century onward. Bede also wrote the *History of the Abbots of Wearmouth and Jarrow*, biblical commentaries, scientific and educational texts, including *On the Art of Metre* and *On the Computation of Time* and multiple *Lives* of Cuthbert (one in rhyming verse). He was also a great monk.

Nothing is known of Bede's parentage. He was born near the end of the seventh century in Northumbria. At the age of seven, he entered the monastery of St Peter and St Paul at Wearmouth and Jarrow. He was ordained a deacon at 19, and a priest at 30, but he never rose above that status. Very little else is known about him; a single autobiographical paragraph, at the end of Book 5 in *The Ecclesiastical History*, tells us not much more than the above.

What we do know, from his writings, is that although Bede was definitely a Roman monk, particularly keen on getting the dating of Easter 'correct', he had a love of the Celtic saints. His *Lives* of Cuthbert and the great accolade given to Aidan in his *Ecclesiastical History*, which reflected Gregory the Great's description of the 'perfect priest', tell us that Bede could see the holy and spiritual depth of these people, and wanted to share it with all, despite having strong opposing views on certain doctrines.

Bede's remains were stolen from their original burial place and taken to where they are now, in Durham Cathedral. On his grave slab at Durham are inscribed the words *HIC SUNT IN FOSSA BEDAE VENERABILIS OSSA* ('Here are buried the bones of the Venerable Bede'). The epitaph was at first unfinished, as those who were creating the slab felt that Bede deserved more than just his name, but couldn't think how to describe him, so they decided to sleep on it. During the night, so legend says, angels came along and inscribed *VENERABILIS* in the gap left on the stone, thus giving Bede the accolade he deserved.

Meditation

Spend a few moments simply resting. Breathe gently and slowly. Become aware of the constant presence of God which envelops you and permeates you.

Bede was someone who desired to share the inspirational lives of many saints. He could see the holiness in these people, and the power of God, despite the fact that he strongly disagreed with certain parts of their theology and teaching.

How do you respond to those of the Christian faith in whom you can see the holiness of God, but who perhaps have theological beliefs that you disagree with? Do you disregard everything they say, and their whole life, because of a few pieces of religious understanding? Or are you able to focus on what you agree with and the qualities within them that inspire you, rather than the disagreements?

Spend time with God now, dwelling upon these questions.

Scripture

'Don't judge, so that you won't be judged. For with whatever judgment you judge, you will be judged; and with whatever measure you measure, it will be measured to you. Why do you see the speck that is in your brother's eye, but don't consider the beam that is in your own eye? Or how will you tell your brother, "Let me remove the speck from your eye;" and behold, the beam is in your own eye? You hypocrite! First remove the beam out of your own eye, and then you can see clearly to remove the speck out of your brother's eye.'

MATTHEW 7:1–5

Blessing

May you be one who tells the stories of others to inspire the people you know.

May you see the holiness within those who are living holy lives, even if not all of their beliefs run in line with your own.

May you focus upon what unites you and others, rather than on the differences that divide you.

5
Boisil

FEAST DAY: 7 July (d.664)

We know very little about Boisil except that he was the prior of Melrose and a teacher and friend of Cuthbert, but he certainly had a great impact on Christian spirituality in the Northumbrian kingdom, not least through his influence over Cuthbert, with whom he developed an *anam chara* (soul friend) relationship.[18]

Boisil often went out walking through the local villages, preaching and teaching about Christ and about living as an authentic Christian. He encouraged people to live out everything he taught them, not just by what he said but by his example. Like many of the great Celtic saints, he preached only what he was already living, not expecting anyone to behave in ways that he himself did not. 'It was the custom amongst the English people at that time, when a clerk or a priest came to a village, for all to gather… to hear the Word, gladly listening to what was said and still more gladly carrying out in their lives whatever they heard and could understand.'[19]

Boisil had a prophetic vision of Cuthbert becoming a bishop, which came true despite the fact that Cuthbert did not want it. When Boisil caught the plague, Cuthbert came and sat at his deathbed, fulfilling Boisil's dying wish to read the Gospel of John with him.

So Boisil died hearing the words of 'the beloved apostle' being read by Cuthbert, and Boisil's influence was not forgotten by Cuthbert, who went on to surpass his master in his own influence on others.

Meditation

Spend a few moments simply resting. Breathe gently and slowly. Become aware of the constant presence of God which envelops you and permeates you.

Boisil was a teacher of great repute. People loved him and his manner. He taught people only what he was living himself.

Each of us has an influence upon others, even if we do not realise it. Whom could you influence? To whom might you be an *anam chara*?

Spend time with God now, dwelling upon these questions.

Scripture

'Don't let your heart be troubled. Believe in God. Believe also in me. In my Father's house are many homes. If it weren't so, I would have told you. I am going to prepare a place for you. If I go and prepare a place for you, I will come again, and will receive you to myself; that where I am, you may be there also. Where I go, you know, and you know the way.'

Thomas said to him, 'Lord, we don't know where you are going. How can we know the way?'

Jesus said to him, 'I am the way, the truth, and the life. No one comes to the Father, except through me. If you had known me, you would have known my Father also. From now on, you know him, and have seen him.'

Philip said to him, 'Lord, show us the Father, and that will be enough for us.'

Jesus said to him, 'Have I been with you such a long time, and do you not know me, Philip? He who has seen me has seen the Father. How do you say, "Show us the Father?" Don't you believe that I am in the Father, and the Father in me? The words that I tell you, I speak not from myself; but the Father who lives in me does his works. Believe me that I am in the Father, and the Father in me; or else believe me for the very works' sake. Most certainly I tell you, he who believes in me, the works that I do, he will do also; and he will do greater works than these, because I am going to my Father.'

JOHN 14:1–12

Blessing

May you know the leading of God in your life, and may you live out your calling.
May you be one who draws others on in their journey with God.
May you know the love of, and of being, an anam chara.

6

Brendan the 'Navigator'

FEAST DAY: 16 May (d.575)

Born in the Munster region of Ireland, Brendan grew up in monasteries and planted more when he was a grown man. He was known as a very spiritual man and the spiritual father of almost 3000 monks.

Brendan embodied the Celtic spirit of adventure: he loved the sea and went on various voyages. Perhaps the most famous was his journey to what is now known as America, nearly 1000 years before Columbus arrived there. Brendan was inspired to take this incredible adventure after listening to the story of Barinthus' sea voyage to 'the island which is called the Promised Land of the Saints'.[20] Brendan took aside a small company of monks to seek their advice. He was determined to make the journey to this Promised Land of the Saints, but asked for their thoughts first. We are told that 'Brendan and those who were with him completed a 40-day fast in three-day periods before they set out'.[21]

The voyage was certainly an adventure. It was not always easy, but presented many dangers. Often the monks found themselves lacking food and drink, with no land in sight. One of the islands they approached sent fear running through Brendan, as he could hear the sound of bellows and the pounding of hammers. One of the savage-looking inhabitants saw the boat full of monks and, with some tongs, threw a massive red-hot piece of slag at it. Brendan urged the monks to row away from the island, but before long the situation got worse:

> All the inhabitants of the island ran down to the shore, each carrying yet more pieces. Some tossed them at the servants of God... They ran back to their forges, setting them on fire, and

soon it appeared that the whole island was one big furnace while the sea boiled like a cooking pot… Even when the island was no longer in sight the wailing of the inhabitants still reached their ears and the stench of the island still filled their nostrils.[22]

There were also some wonderful encounters and moments of God's grace and protection, because 'God wished to show [Brendan] his many wonders in the great ocean'.[23] On one occasion, when they had been at sea for 40 days since their last harbour, 'they saw a creature of immense size following them at a distance; it blew spray from its nostrils and cut through the waves at high speed as if coming to devour them'.[24] Three times the monks raised a cry to God to save them, and Brendan encouraged them to have faith in God.

Another sea monster… rushed to meet the first [and]… immediately attacked it. The old man [Brendan] said to his brothers, 'See, my sons, the wonderful deeds of our Redeemer. See how the beasts obey their Creator. The matter will soon be over, and you will not be harmed by this battle in any way, but it will be remembered as having been to the glory of God.'[25]

The second monster tore the first into three pieces, then swam away. Some days later, the monks arrived at an island. At the place where they harboured their boat, they found one-third of the sea monster, and sat together and ate it. Brendan returned from his successful voyage, back to his home, where he was welcomed with great joy.

The journey that Brendan took has been proven possible,[26] and the documentation that charts the journey has been shown to describe real physical places; for example, 'tall pillars of glass towering out of the sea' are recorded on his journey when he would have been passing glaciers and icebergs.

Shall I abandon, O King of mysteries, the soft comforts of home?
Shall I turn my back on my native land and my face towards the sea?
Shall I put myself wholly at the mercy of God?

Shall I leave the prints of my knees on the sandy beach?
A record of my final prayer in my native land.
Shall I take my tiny coracle across the wide sparkling ocean?
O King of the glorious heaven, shall I go of my own choice upon
the sea?
O Christ, help me on the wild waves!
PRAYER OF BRENDAN

Meditation

Spend a few moments simply resting. Breathe gently and slowly. Become aware of the constant presence of God which envelops you and permeates you.

Life can be an adventure, and our journey with God is an adventure. Let us face our adventures with the same passion that set Brendan apart from others, and with an excitement that God is drawing us on in life.

What is your inner journey like—the one you are on in your life? How much do you allow God to take control of it? Are you on a self-driven journey or are you on a divine adventure?

We all face times in our lives when we must 'put out to sea', leaving the comfort of the known, our 'native land', to face the unknown and venture into what may be turbulent waters. Are you willing to trust God as you join his adventure?

Spend time with God now, dwelling upon these questions.

Scripture

This is the history of the generations of Noah: Noah was a righteous man, blameless among the people of his time. Noah walked with God. Noah became the father of three sons: Shem, Ham, and Japheth. The earth was corrupt before God, and the earth was filled with violence. God saw the earth, and saw that it was corrupt, for all flesh had corrupted their way on the earth.

God said to Noah, 'I will bring an end to all flesh, for the earth is filled with violence through them. Behold, I will destroy them and the earth. Make a ship of gopher wood. You shall make rooms in the ship, and shall seal it inside and outside with pitch. This is how you shall make it. The length of the ship shall be three hundred cubits, its width fifty cubits, and its height thirty cubits. You shall make a roof in the ship, and you shall finish it to a cubit upward. You shall set the door of the ship in its side. You shall make it with lower, second, and third levels. I, even I, do bring the flood of waters on this earth, to destroy all flesh having the breath of life from under the sky. Everything that is in the earth will die. But I will establish my covenant with you. You shall come into the ship, you, your sons, your wife, and your sons' wives with you. Of every living thing of all flesh, you shall bring two of every sort into the ship, to keep them alive with you. They shall be male and female. Of the birds after their kind, of the livestock after their kind, of every creeping thing of the ground after its kind, two of every sort will come to you, to keep them alive. Take with you of all food that is eaten, and gather it to yourself; and it will be for food for you, and for them.' Thus Noah did. He did all that God commanded him.

GENESIS 6:9–22

Blessing

May you be willing to set out on the path to which God calls you.
May you know the adventure and protection of a life with God.
May you be willing to do all that God asks of you, even if you cannot understand it or have no control over it.

7
Brigið

FEAST DAY: 1 February (d.525)

The feast day of Brigid of Kildare, celebrated just before the Christian festival of lights, is also the first day of Imbolc (meaning something like 'Ewe's milk'), the beginning of the Celtic season of spring, passing from the darkness of the season of death (winter) and celebrating the coming of new life. Imbolc is a very feminine festival, with great emphasis on the importance of women in the community.

Brigid of Kildare was well known as an embodiment of the Celtic traditions of both the *anam chara* (she is famed for saying that 'a person without an *anam chara* is like a body without a head') and generosity.

When Brigid was a young girl, her father was so afraid that she would make the family bankrupt by giving everything away that he tried to marry her off to a local chieftain. He took her to the chieftain in a beautiful carriage, and left her in it while he went to find the man. As a sign of respect and peace to the chieftain, Brigid's father left his sword in the carriage. While Brigid waited, a beggar came along, asking for alms. Brigid's heart burst with compassion when she saw him, but she said she had nothing to give. As the beggar turned to leave, Brigid remembered her father's sword with its gold-covered scabbard. Calling the beggar back, she gave the sword away.

On the father's return, he saw that his sword had gone and Brigid explained everything. When the chieftain understood that Brigid would also give away everything he owned, he refused to take her in marriage. Brigid's father, at the end of his tether, allowed Brigid to leave and become a bride of Christ, which was all she had wanted.[27]

Brigid was known as a spiritual midwife. Born in Ireland around the time that Patrick died, she is famous for being the person who 'brought Christianity up' in Ireland, after Patrick had brought it to birth there.

Brigid is also known for her great heart towards all who were spiritually open, and her many encounters with such people, including druids. One famous story tells how she nursed a pagan chief to health and taught him about the love of Christ by weaving a cross from reeds. The 'Brigid cross' is a lovely interwoven square cross that many people put in places that are not used over the winter but will be used much in the spring and summer, as a blessing to that place and the earth.[28]

Meditation

Spend a few moments simply resting. Breathe gently and slowly. Become aware of the constant presence of God which envelops you and permeates you.

Brigid was a person with great generosity of heart, who saw the need of all, great and lowly, and desired to give them all she could. She saw the importance of total dedication to God in all she did, and believed that no one, despite what they themselves might have thought, was beyond her help.

How do you express the generosity of God? Does your heart of generosity extend more toward people you know, or those who are Christians, than it does toward strangers and people of other faiths?

Spend time with God now, dwelling upon these questions.

Scripture

He, desiring to justify himself, asked Jesus, 'Who is my neighbour?'

Jesus answered, 'A certain man was going down from Jerusalem to Jericho, and he fell among robbers, who both stripped him and beat him, and departed, leaving him half dead. By chance a certain priest was going down that way. When he saw him, he passed by on the other side. In the same way a Levite also, when he came to the place, and saw him, passed by on the other side. But a certain Samaritan, as he travelled, came where he was. When he saw him, he was moved with compassion, came to him, and bound up his wounds, pouring on oil and wine. He set him on his own animal, and brought him to an inn, and took care of him. On the next day, when he departed, he took out two denarii, and gave them to the host, and said to him, "Take care of him. Whatever you spend beyond that, I will repay you when I return." Now which of these three do you think seemed to be a neighbour to him who fell among the robbers?'

He said, 'He who showed mercy on him.'

Then Jesus said to him, 'Go and do likewise.'
LUKE 10:29–37

Blessing

May you know the generosity of God poured out upon you.
May you not only receive God's generosity, but also be a channel
*   for it to flow out into the world.*
May you express this generosity without distinction, to stranger
*   and friend.*

8

Cadfan

FEAST DAY: 1 November (d. early sixth century)

Cadfan was a British monk who went to live in Brittany but, later in life, moved back to Wales where he had grown up. It is possible that he was at Illtyd's monastery in Llanilltyd Fawr, along with David, Gildas and Samson.

Cadfan founded a Christian centre, a *clas*, in the place now called Llangadfan, named after him. He is also reputed to have been the first monk to plant any kind of settlement on Bardsey Island and consecrate it as holy ground. The island is now said to house the remains of over 20,000 saints, as well as being the place where the restless spirit of Merlin dwells, waiting to raise King Arthur in Britain's darkest hour.

On Cadfan's journey back to Wales from Brittany, he was accompanied by (among others) Baglan, Flewyn, Gredifael, Tanwg, Twrog, Tegai, Trillo, Tecwyn and Llechid—the children of Ithel Hael, an Armorican prince. These nine boys and girls had been so enamoured of and inspired by the Spirit of God that dwelt within Cadfan, which they had seen at work both within him and through him, that they went with him to learn more. All of them became missionaries and church planters right across Wales, and so continued the influence of Cadfan for generations to come.

These nine brothers and sisters themselves are worth studying.

Meditation

Spend a few moments simply resting. Breathe gently and slowly. Become aware of the constant presence of God which envelops you and permeates you.

Cadfan left his homeland and became a holy teacher to people in a different place. He embodied such a deep sense of holiness that an entire generation of a royal family followed him, laying down their upbringing (with the blessing of their father) and becoming missionaries in a land new to them.

As you live your life, what is it that you give to the next generation? What inspiration do you provide for those growing up in both life and the faith?

Spend time with God now, dwelling upon these questions.

Scripture

Hear my teaching, my people.
Turn your ears to the words of my mouth.
I will open my mouth in a parable.
I will utter dark sayings of old,
Which we have heard and known,
and our fathers have told us.
We will not hide them from their children,
telling to the generation to come the praises of Yahweh,
his strength, and his wondrous deeds that he has done.
For he established a testimony in Jacob,
and appointed a teaching in Israel,
which he commanded our fathers,
that they should make them known to their children;

that the generation to come might know, even the children who
*   should be born;*
*   who should arise and tell their children,*
that they might set their hope in God,
*   and not forget God's deeds,*
*   but keep his commandments.*
PSALM 78:1–7

Blessing

May you know the inspiration of God in your life.
May you live a life that others can aspire to.
May you pass on the understanding you gain to the next generation,
*   so that they will grow to inspire others.*

9
Cadoc

FEAST DAY: 25 September (d.577)

Cadoc was the son of Gwynllyw ap Glywys, a princeling of Gwent. Brought up as a member of the warrior class, Cadoc refused to lead his father's men when he gained the right to lead. The Irish monk Tathan, living in Caerwent, had given Cadoc his early education. Through this, Cadoc learned of the spiritual battle and thereafter put all his understanding of military leadership into spiritual war instead of physical land wars.

Cadoc founded his first monastery at Llancarfan in the Vale of Glamorgan, and from there he went to Ireland to study for three years. Returning to Wales via Scotland, he studied with Bachan, a teacher of rhetoric from Italy.

Cadoc is known for his missionary activity, demonstrating the love of Christ through word and deed throughout the countryside of south Wales. He became a hermit in the hills of Wales, where many came to visit him and were inspired by his wisdom and spiritual prowess. He was also instrumental in the conversion of Illtyd, founder of the most important monastic teaching centre in early medieval Britain, where David, Gildas, Samson and many others gained their education.

Cadoc taught Illtyd, who was also a warrior before meeting him, what it meant to be a warrior for Christ rather than among men, fighting for the King of kings in the spiritual battle, both within one's self and in the outside world (see Chapter 25).

Meditation

Spend a few moments simply resting. Breathe gently and slowly. Become aware of the constant presence of God which envelops you and permeates you.

Cadoc knew that life included battle—times of struggle. He knew the reality of the spiritual realm and the battle we face as we live out a Christ-like life for God.

How do you see the battle? How do you view the difficult times? Do you try to 'go it alone' or are you willing to fall on the power and help of God?

Spend time with God now, dwelling upon these questions.

Scripture

Finally, be strong in the Lord, and in the strength of his might. Put on the whole armour of God, that you may be able to stand against the wiles of the devil. For our wrestling is not against flesh and blood, but against the principalities, against the powers, against the world's rulers of the darkness of this age, and against the spiritual forces of wickedness in the heavenly places. Therefore put on the whole armour of God, that you may be able to withstand in the evil day, and, having done all, to stand. Stand therefore, having the utility belt of truth buckled around your waist, and having put on the breastplate of righteousness, and having fitted your feet with the preparation of the Good News of peace; above all, taking up the shield of faith, with which you will be able to quench all the fiery darts of the evil one. And take the helmet of salvation, and the sword of the Spirit, which is the word of God; with all prayer and requests, praying at all times in the Spirit, and being watchful to this end in all perseverance and requests for all the saints.

EPHESIANS 6:10–18

Blessing

May you know the strength and surrounding protection of God with you today.

May you know God's aid in the difficult times and during spiritual attack.

May you know the reality of the work of spiritual darkness without seeing 'a demon behind every bush'.

10

Cædmon (Bard of Christ)

FEAST DAY: 11 February (d.680)

One of the marks of Celtic Christianity was not to destroy the culture of the people when bringing the message of Christ to a new place, but to put Christ at the centre of all things.

An important element of Celtic culture was the singing and storytelling in the mead halls. Bede tells us that in Whitby Abbey, run by Hilda, the tradition of gathering for the 'passing of the harp' (for storytelling, poetry and song) was a part of community life there.[29] Cædmon (Kadmon), a shy cowherd in Hilda's Whitby compound, would run away and hide each time he had to 'share the harp' in these community gatherings, as he could not sing or tell a story well. When the harp was on its way to him, he would sneak out and go home or back to the cowshed. One night, in the cowshed, he had a dream of an angel telling him to sing the story of creation. In the morning, Cædmon could remember the song. He sang as he went about his day, and more songs and stories came to him. Heard by others and eventually by Hilda, Cædmon shared his new gift with the people.

Cædmon's songs and stories were all in the language of the Angles, rather than in Latin as was most common. His stories were, for the first time, for the common native Angles. He became known as the 'Bard of Christ to the English', being the first to tell the stories of the Bible in his native 'English' (Anglian) tongue, inspired by his continuing visionary dreams. His story is, fittingly, shared through poetry here, as he is the patron saint of poetry and poets:

The first of English poets he,
Who nurtured by the Whitby sea
A poor and simple cowherd seemed.
Yet here the gold of poetry gleamed
Though hidden deep within his soul
For from the company he stole
Fearful to be found afraid
When they their entertainment made
The very least among the throng
With little speech nor any song.
Then in the stillness of one night
His soul was filled with heavenly light
A vision of the world being made
Of God's creation all displayed.
As in the stable stall he lay
Dreaming he heard an angel pray
And speak to him of God's great world
And how its majesty unfurled.
Then day by day to his inspired mind
That had seemed deaf and dumb and blind
There came sweet words so bright and clear.
Then Mother Hilda came to hear
stayed with all her Abbey folk
While Cædmon, poet of Whitby, spoke.
No longer now to steal away
When came his turn the harp to play
For in his Saxon mother tongue
Were all his splendid verses sung
And improvised with great delight
In many a stormy winter's night
When firelight filled the raftered hall
In far off ancient Streonshalh.
Then folk would learn the poems by heart
Or memorise a favourite part
Making them one with Christian praise
In those remote, unlettered days.[30]

Meditation

Spend a few moments simply resting. Breathe gently and slowly. Become aware of the constant presence of God which envelops you and permeates you.

Cædmon was someone who knew his human limits but was willing to go beyond them when the Spirit of God intervened. He recognised the divine presence within his dream and stepped out boldly in the spiritual gifting which he had received.

How willing are you to step out and do things for which God may give you the gifting, which you may have previously thought were not within your own ability? Are you one who would continue to run away, or would you step out in faith and do what God seems to be calling you to do?

Spend time with God now, dwelling upon these questions.

Scripture

Jacob lived in the land of his father's travels, in the land of Canaan. This is the history of the generations of Jacob. Joseph, being seventeen years old, was feeding the flock with his brothers. He was a boy with the sons of Bilhah and Zilpah, his father's wives. Joseph brought an evil report of them to their father. Now Israel loved Joseph more than all his children, because he was the son of his old age, and he made him a coat of many colours. His brothers saw that their father loved him more than all his brothers, and they hated him, and couldn't speak peaceably to him.

Joseph dreamed a dream, and he told it to his brothers, and they hated him all the more. He said to them, 'Please hear this dream which I have dreamed: for behold, we were binding sheaves in the field, and behold, my sheaf arose and also stood upright; and behold, your sheaves came around, and bowed down to my sheaf.'

His brothers said to him, 'Will you indeed reign over us? Or will you indeed have dominion over us?' They hated him all the more for his dreams and for his words. He dreamed yet another dream, and told it to his brothers, and said, 'Behold, I have dreamed yet another dream: and behold, the sun and the moon and eleven stars bowed down to me.' He told it to his father and to his brothers. His father rebuked him, and said to him, 'What is this dream that you have dreamed? Will I and your mother and your brothers indeed come to bow ourselves down to you to the earth?' His brothers envied him, but his father kept this saying in mind.

GENESIS 37:1–11

Blessing

May the gifts of God flow through you, out into the world.
May you be open to God's use of you to fulfil all your dormant unused gifts.
May you never limit what God wants to do through you, by your own fear of what you think you cannot do.

II

Cedd

FEAST DAY: 26 October (d.664)

Cedd was 'a wise, holy, and upright man'[31] and, along with his brothers, Chad, Cynibil and Caelin, was trained on Lindisfarne by Bishop Finan. He became a kind of personal missionary to the king of Northumbria, King Oswiu. When the king of the Middle Angles (within the old kingdom of Mercia) wanted Christian missionaries, Oswiu sent Cedd and some others. Later, the king of the East Saxons (from which we get the county name Essex) also wanted a mission team from Northumbria, so Oswiu called Cedd back to take one other monk with him and go to preach and teach the East Saxons. St Peter's Chapel in Bradwell-on-Sea, Essex, was built in 654 by Cedd and local helpers, and, at the time of writing, is still in use.

Cedd returned to Lindisfarne to report to Finan (and probably Oswiu) on how the mission was going. When he reported that the work was progressing well and the mission was a great success, Finan made him the bishop of the East Saxons and sent him back with blessings. Cedd took with him the monastic Rule which he had learned from Lindisfarne, bringing Celtic Christianity down to Essex.

Cedd often returned to Northumbria to preach and continue his involvement in the Christian mission there. He attended the Synod of Whitby in 664, acting as an interpreter in the debate.[32] On an earlier occasion, while visiting Northumbria, Cedd was offered land on which to build a monastic centre. He chose some land within a mountainous area, which was thought to be a place of robbers and cut-throats. He spent the 40-day season of Lent in prayer and fasting within the hills, to cleanse the area.

Every day except Sunday he prolonged his fast until evening as his custom was and then he took nothing but a small quantity of bread, one hen's egg, and a little milk mixed with water... When the work of fasting and prayer was ended, he built a monastery there, now called Lastingham.[33]

Many years passed and Cedd was very successful in his mission from Lastingham, but the place became subject to plague, of which Cedd died. After his death, his brother Chad took charge of the monastic centre.

Meditation

Spend a few moments simply resting. Breathe gently and slowly. Become aware of the constant presence of God which envelops you and permeates you.

Cedd was willing to be sent wherever the king wanted him to go. He took with him the life and Rule with which he had grown in the faith, and became a trusted and influential person. He was deeply trusted by all, as is shown by the trust placed in him to play the part of interpreter at the Synod of Whitby.

How willing are you to follow the direction of those you class as your spiritual leaders? What if they wanted to send you somewhere (not necessarily physically) that you might find hard? Would you go?

Who do you have as your spiritual 'leader', other than Christ?

Spend time with God now, dwelling upon these questions.

Scripture

Remember your leaders, men who spoke to you the word of God, and considering the results of their conduct, imitate their faith. Jesus Christ is the same yesterday, today, and forever. Don't be carried away by various and strange teachings, for it is good that the heart be established by grace, not by food, through which those who were so occupied were not benefited…

Through [Christ], then, let us offer up a sacrifice of praise to God continually, that is, the fruit of lips which proclaim allegiance to his name. But don't forget to be doing good and sharing, for with such sacrifices God is well pleased.

Obey your leaders and submit to them, for they watch on behalf of your souls, as those who will give account, that they may do this with joy, and not with groaning, for that would be unprofitable for you.

HEBREWS 13:7–9, 15–17

Blessing

May you know the guidance of God through those who lead you.
May you be willing to follow God's direction given through them.
May you be one who hears the voice of God, to be able to guide
*   others in the right way.*

12

Ciaran

FEAST DAY: 9 September (d.545)

Ciaran was a descendant of a national Bard of Ireland. Legend says that Patrick, Bridget and Columba all prophesied about Ciaran's coming. When he was yet in his mother's womb, even the king's druid said of him, 'As the sun shines among the stars of heaven, so he will shine on earth in miracles and marvels that cannot be told. Lord, you foretold his birth by prophets, even as Isaac's birth was foretold to Abraham.'

One of these marvels, so the story goes, happened when a group of disgruntled thugs set a wild dog on Ciaran to tear him apart. As the dog ran towards him, snarling and barking, it is said that Ciaran stood calmly and recited Psalm 20:7–8 ('Some trust in chariots, and some in horses, but we trust the name of Yahweh our God. They are bowed down and fallen, but we rise up, and stand upright'), whereupon the dog lay down, quiet and still.

Ciaran was one of the twelve apostles of Ireland trained at Clonard. After his training, Ciaran established his own monastic centres, which drew many people to them and to the Christ he followed.

Following a prophetic vision of Ciaran as a great fruitful tree planted by a river in the centre of Ireland—seen by both Ciaran himself and his soul friend, Enda—he established a Community of God at Clonmacnoise. As Ciaran and a few other monks were placing the first poles of the church at Clonmacnoise, Dermot, a prince on the run, came across them. Intrigued, he asked what they were doing. Ciaran replied that they were 'building a little church'. Dermot, being a kind and vigorous man, joined in and helped. Ciaran, touched by the humility of this prince, prophesied that the kingdom would belong to Dermot by the same time tomorrow. 'How can this be,' asked Dermot, 'as Tuathal rules over Ireland and I am in exile?'

'The "how" is a matter for God,' said Ciaran, and left it at that.

A pagan companion of Dermot overheard the conversation and immediately took it upon himself to go to Tuathal alone, under the pretence of peace. Once there, he thrust his spear into the king, killing him. The pagan was instantly killed by the king's men, but Dermot was accepted as king at Tara the next day, just as Ciaran had said.[34] Dermot ruled as a Christian king, and was buried at Clonmacnoise.

The opening of the church at Clonmacnoise drew two warring tribes to peace and unity. Such an incredible feat was this peace that Clonmacnoise instantly became known for the presence and peace of God. The community there lasted 1000 years, and its location is still one of the most visited sacred sites in Ireland, even though Ciaran died of plague only seven months after establishing it.

Ciaran was a man who saw the grace and glory of God in the ordinary things of life, blessing such things as the dye used for clothes.

Meditation

Spend a few moments simply resting. Breathe gently and slowly. Become aware of the constant presence of God which envelops you and permeates you.

Ciaran trained under a wise teacher and moved in the spiritual gifts of God. He trusted God in all things and saw the presence of God in ordinary life, from blessing dye to calming a wild dog.

How do you perceive God in the everyday parts of life? Is God put aside for 'spiritual' times, or is he a part of your housework, office work, or whatever it is you do?

Spend time with God now, dwelling upon these questions.

Scripture

Some trust in chariots, and some in horses,
but we trust the name of Yahweh our God.
They are bowed down and fallen,
but we rise up, and stand upright.
PSALM 20:7–8

Blessing

May you draw others to Christ simply by who you are.
May you trust in God more than your own strength.
May you know and express the presence of God in the ordinary
and everyday.

13

Colman

FEAST DAY: 18 February (d.676)

Colman, a man of 'innate prudence',[35] was bishop of Lindisfarne at
the time of the Synod of Whitby, and attended the synod as one of
the representatives of the Celtic (Irish) Church. Colman was the first to
speak and give account of the Irish ways and where they originated.
Colman spoke of the apostle John, 'the disciple who the Lord specially
loved… [the apostle]… who was reckoned worthy to recline on the
breast of the Lord [and] all the world acknowledges his wisdom',[36] and
how the Irish (Celtic) customs, especially the dating of Easter, came
from the teachings of the communities of this beloved apostle. When
Colman had finished speaking, Agilbert from the Roman contingent
was invited to speak, but he asked Wilfrid to speak instead. King Oswiu
listened to both sides and finally made the decision (based on the fear
of not being let into heaven by Peter) that all of Britain should abide by
the Roman rules and dates.

Colman, saddened 'that his teachings were rejected and his principles
despised… took those who wished to follow him… and returned to
Ireland in order to discuss with his own party what he ought to do in
the matter'.[37]

Colman had great devotion to his beliefs and the way he had been
taught to live out the Christian faith. He decided that he would find it
too hard to change his way of life after the Synod of Whitby, but instead
of fighting back or refusing to obey the king's decree, in humility he
stepped out of the role he loved in the place he loved, giving it to
someone else. Then he went, with others, to discern what would be the
best and most godly response and life-decision.

Meditation

Spend a few moments simply resting. Breathe gently and slowly. Become aware of the constant presence of God which envelops you and permeates you.

Colman was a man of God who loved to serve the Lord and was dedicated to the way of life he had been taught. But he was also humble and righteous, knowing that retreating for a time of discernment was godlier than fighting back.

How do you respond when decisions don't go your way? Do you react with emotional outbursts, or do you step back and take time to discern what might be the right thing to do? How might you live in such an awareness of God that you more often respond in the right way than with an unhelpful outburst?

Spend time with God now, dwelling upon these questions.

Scripture

'When they bring you before the synagogues, the rulers, and the authorities, don't be anxious how or what you will answer, or what you will say; for the Holy Spirit will teach you in that same hour what you must say.'
LUKE 12:11–12

Blessing

May you know the leading of God in your life.
May you live a life dwelling in the divine presence.
May you always respond in a godly way and find space for
    discernment when things do not go the way you want them to.

14
Columba

FEAST DAY: 9 June (d.597)

Columba was born into the nobility in the north of Ireland, possibly in line to be the High King of Ireland. He was well known as an organiser, poet/song writer, and prophet. He planted a great many monasteries in Ireland before being involved in a dispute over copyright while he was at the monastery in Clonard, under Finnian. As part of his creative meditations, Columba copied out the book of Psalms from Finnian's own handwritten copy. When Columba was due to leave, he wished to take his copy of the Psalms with him, but, as he had copied Finnian's personal margin notes as well, Finnian was not happy for the book to leave Clonard. A legal battle followed, in which the High King of Ireland, Diarmait mac Cerbhiall, decided that Columba's copy was to stay in Clonard. The dispute escalated into military battle and, as a result, when the battle was over, Columba was banished from Ireland. He vowed to convert as many souls to Christ as there were soldiers who had lost their lives in the copyright battle.

Columba sailed from the north coast of Ireland to the Irish-owned part of what we now call Scotland.[38] He landed on other isles before settling on Iona, a place from which he could not see his beloved Ireland— knowing that if he lived on an isle where he could see Ireland, he would be too tempted to return.

On Iona, Columba founded what became his most famous monastery and mission centre. It was from here, around a generation after Columba died, that Aidan was sent to Lindisfarne and became the 'apostle to the English'; many others, too, gained their training in Iona.

Columba was well known for going away for long periods of time to pray and converse with angels, and many of these encounters were witnessed by other monks on Iona, who saw the angels with Columba. On one occasion, when he shut himself in a hut for a length of time, blinding light could be seen through the cracks in the door and through the keyhole. His face is reported to have shone when he had been with God, just as the face of Moses did (Exodus 34:29–35).

Columba's prophetic visions were famous, and were not just about telling the future. On one occasion, he sat writing in his hut on Iona when his countenance suddenly changed and he shouted, 'Help! help!' Two monks who were near the open door were alarmed and asked, 'Why do you cry out?' Columba told them, 'I have directed the angel of the Lord, who was just now standing among you, to go quickly and help one of the monks who has fallen from the top of a roof in the Plain of the Oak Wood' [perhaps Durrow]. The monks were astonished. 'How wonderful beyond words,' Columba went on, 'is the swift motion of an angel; it is as swift as lightning. For the heavenly spirit who flew from us when that man began to fall was there to support him in a twinkling of an eye, before his body reached the ground. How wonderful that help through angels can happen, through such stretches of land and sea which lie between.' Later, they learned that a man had indeed fallen from that great height, but he had broken no bones and did not even feel a bruise.[39]

The Spirit of God was upon Columba greatly. He was a great prophet, teacher, leader and miracle worker, as well as being known for seeing God in creation.

Meditation

Spend a few moments simply resting. Breathe gently and slowly. Become aware of the constant presence of God which envelops you and permeates you.

Columba's prophetic ministry and angelic encounters came through his prolonged and regular practice of withdrawing from the busy life of the monastery and mission work to engage in contemplative prayer.

How much time do you spend in contemplative prayer? This is not a speaking type of prayer (audibly or internally), but a dwelling in the divine presence, a resting with the beloved, a 'prolonged immersion in the rivers of tranquillity which flow from God into the whole universe and draw all things back to God'.[40]

In what ways might you be able to deepen your times of stillness with God? How might it increase your ability to hear God's voice and encounter angels?

Spend time with God now, dwelling upon these questions.

Scripture

But whoever keeps his word, God's love has most certainly been perfected in him. This is how we know that we are in him: he who says he remains in him ought himself also to walk just like [Christ] walked.
1 JOHN 2:5–6

But Jesus often withdrew to lonely places and prayed.
LUKE 5:16 (NIV)

Blessing

May you, like Columba, seek to do good, even from the results of wrong.
May you be so drawn into the presence of God that your face shines from his presence.
May you be a great inspiration for others in their walk with God.

15
Columbanus

FEAST DAY: 23 November (d.615)

Born in southern Ireland, Columbanus came from a Christian family and was handsome, fair and well educated. He had everything the world could offer, but there was a sense within him of something lacking. His heart was moved and he decided that he wanted to follow God for himself, not just because of his upbringing.

Columbanus went to the local wise hermit. Her prophetic vision told him what he needed: 'Flee! Flee that temptation [of money and a rich life]. Don't think you can conquer it. Go!'[41] Columbanus was to give up all his material possessions and security and throw his lot in with God. He immediately went home to pack his things. His mother was so distraught that she lay across the threshold, but he was so convinced of God's call that he stepped over her, said goodbye and left.

Columbanus trained at the great monastery in Bangor in Northern Ireland, but felt called to wander and plant other communities of God. He travelled the continent of Europe, establishing major monasteries that were run according to his rule of life. Although this rule was quite hard, and many of Columbanus' monasteries later adopted the gentler rule of Benedict, his teachings were never completely abandoned.

The final monastery that Columbanus established was at Bobbio in present-day Italy, where he died. Bobbio maintained the rule of Columbanus and many of the Celtic styles of Christianity, including Columbanus' love of animals and care for creation, as a major part of its teaching. Columbanus is credited with saying, 'If you want to know the Creator, you must first know his creation.'

Many years later, the teachings and monks of Bobbio are thought to have influenced a young man named Francis, from the city of Assisi Having left the military and the life of a troubadour, Francis was determined to live a life for God. He quite possibly learned some of what he included in his own rule of life from the rule and life of Columbanus.

Meditation

Spend a few moments simply resting. Breathe gently and slowly. Become aware of the constant presence of God which envelops you and permeates you.

Columbanus was a man who understood the importance and benefit of spiritual disciplines. He practisded them and taught them, and integrated them into the whole of life. The Celtic Christians called this process 'green martyrdom', but it was not a self-persecuting asceticism; it was a dedication to spiritual fitness.[42]

What spiritual disciplines do you have in place in your life? What might need changing or adding? How might structure in your spiritual life, like a trellis for a garden plant, aid your growth in God?

Spend time with God now, dwelling upon these questions.

Scripture

Now this is the commandment, the statutes, and the ordinances, which Yahweh your God commanded to teach you, that you might do them in the land where you go over to possess it; that you might fear Yahweh your God, to keep all his statutes and his commandments, which I command you; you, and your son, and your son's son, all the days of your life; and that your days may be prolonged. Hear therefore, Israel, and observe to do it; that it may be well with you, and that you may increase mightily, as

Yahweh, the God of your fathers, has promised to you, in a land flowing with milk and honey. Hear, Israel: Yahweh is our God. Yahweh is one. You shall love Yahweh your God with all your heart, with all your soul, and with all your might. These words, which I command you today, shall be on your heart; and you shall teach them diligently to your children, and shall talk of them when you sit in your house, and when you walk by the way, and when you lie down, and when you rise up. You shall bind them for a sign on your hand, and they shall be for frontlets between your eyes. You shall write them on the door posts of your house, and on your gates.

DEUTERONOMY 6:1–9

Blessing

May you know the joy of walking closely with God.
May you know the blessing of maintaining a routine of spiritual fitness.
May the way of life you live be an inspiration to others.

16
Comgall

FEAST DAY: 10 May (d.c.602)

Comgall was first a hermit, dwelling with God in stillness, quietness, contemplation and preparation, before he founded the monastic centre at Bangor, the largest Christian centre in Ireland. Over 3000 monks at a time stayed there, a number which at one time included Columbanus.

Comgall's rule was strict and ascetical. Although we do not have any written rule from within his lifetime, we do have 'The Rule of Comgall', written around three generations after his death, which is thought to closely reflect the life and teachings of the community that Comgall ran.

The rule begins with an encouragement to stick closely to the spiritual disciplines 'of the gentle Lord' laid out in the rule, the first instruction being 'to love Christ, to shun wealth (greed), to remain close to the heavenly king, and to be gentle towards people'.[43] The rule of Comgall also says that 'tepid and lukewarm repentance following a grave sin will not have a great reward in heaven' and that 'whosoever walks the path of repentance would advance a step every day'.[44]

One of the rule's suggestions about prayer says, 'Do not practise long-drawn-out (fat or swollen) devotions, but rather give yourself to prayer at intervals, as you would to food. Pious humbug is an invention of the devil.'[45]

Meditation

Spend a few moments simply resting. Breathe gently and slowly. Become aware of the constant presence of God which envelops you and permeates you.

Having and following a rule, or way of life, is something that helps us in our daily life with God. Like setting up a trellis for a garden plant, dedicating ourselves to a way of life gives structure and support to the freedom of our growth.

Comgall first spent time in contemplative solitude, dwelling in the divine presence, before he stepped out and founded a monastic centre. He created a rule that helped people become closer to God and inspired righteous living. He encouraged regular self-inspection and complete repentance, enabling people to advance one step at a time, each day, to become more Christ-like.

How often do you spend time with God in self-inspection? How often do you repent of the things you have done which may be obstructing your relationship with God? Is there anything within you now which you need to lay before God and repent of?

Spend time with God now, dwelling upon these questions.

Scripture

This is the message which we have heard from him and announce to you, that God is light, and in him is no darkness at all. If we say that we have fellowship with him and walk in the darkness, we lie, and don't tell the truth. But if we walk in the light, as he is in the light, we have fellowship with one another, and the blood of Jesus Christ, his Son, cleanses us from all sin. If we say that we have no sin, we deceive ourselves, and the truth is not in us. If we confess our sins, he is faithful and righteous to forgive us the

sins, and to cleanse us from all unrighteousness. If we say that we haven't sinned, we make him a liar, and his word is not in us.
1 JOHN 1:5–10

Blessing

May you know a deep sense of divine peace within you.
May God show you the things that hinder your walk with him.
May you know the restoration to righteousness that comes from true repentance.

17
Cuthbert

FEAST DAY: 20 March (d.687)

Cuthbert was a prophetic visionary mystic. When out on a hillside in northern Britain one night, sitting with shepherds tending sheep, he had a vision of angels in the sky and glorious light descending from heaven. As the angels went back into heaven, Cuthbert could see that they were carrying the soul of a beloved saint with them. Cuthbert later discovered that he had witnessed the angels carrying the soul of Aidan, founder of Lindisfarne, up to heaven the night he had died.

Having gone through different avenues of training, with much evidence of a powerful life filled with action and contemplation, Cuthbert went to lead the people on Lindisfarne. Although he was a man of action and mission, he desired the quiet stillness of contemplative time with God, so he built a small cell on an island off Lindisfarne. Just outside the ruins standing on the islet today, barely visible, is a round mound of earth, which is quite possibly the place where Cuthbert's cell would have been. But this location turned out to be too close at hand, as the brothers would row out from Lindisfarne to him or call to him from the shore. He decided to go to the Farne islands, a few miles down the coast. As he set out, the locals said that he would never be able to settle on the islands as they were inhabited by demons. Cuthbert spent the first part of his time there in prayer and spiritual battle, and soon the islands were clear of all spiritual influence except for God's.

Cuthbert was famed for preaching and miracle working, and for encountering demonic forces and sending them packing, as mentioned above. On one occasion, he was preaching the word of God in a village when he saw demonic figures approaching. Undeterred, he continued to speak. The demons caused flames of fire to be visible on the roofs of the houses in the village, and the villagers took up containers of water to try to extinguish the fires. Throughout the commotion Cuthbert continued to preach, holding some villagers back to listen. The water was having no effect (little wonder, as the flames were spiritual and not physical). Cuthbert paused in his flow of teaching, rebuked the demons and demanded, in Jesus' name, that the fires be extinguished. At that moment 'the author of lies was put to flight, carrying with him his phantom fires into the empty air'.[46]

Without stumbling over any words, Cuthbert continued teaching the gospel of Christ and 'the crowd… approaching the man of God again, prayed on bended knees to be forgiven for their fickleness of mind, confessing that they realised that the devil never ceased, even for an hour, from hindering the work of man's salvation. And [Cuthbert], affirming the weak and inconstant, continued his interrupted discourse on the way of life.'[47]

Meditation

Spend a few moments simply resting. Breathe gently and slowly. Become aware of the constant presence of God which envelops you and permeates you.

Cuthbert was a man who moved in the power of God. He was acutely aware of the supernatural. He saw into the spirit realms with mystical visions of angels and demons, and overcame dark spiritual forces by expressing the power of God that flowed through him.

You have the same power of God flowing through you. How do you make a stand against the forces of spiritual darkness? Are there things within your life now that need to be overcome?

Spend time with God now, dwelling upon these questions.

Scripture

And being found in human form, he humbled himself, becoming obedient to death, yes, the death of the cross. Therefore God also highly exalted him, and gave to him the name which is above every name; that at the name of Jesus every knee should bow, of those in heaven, those on earth, and those under the earth, and that every tongue should confess that Jesus Christ is Lord, to the glory of God the Father.

PHILIPPIANS 2:8–11

Blessing

May the power of the living God fill you and protect you.
May the power of God flow through you.
May you, in the name of Jesus, overcome any influence of spiritual darkness affecting you.

18

David

FEAST DAY: 1 March (d.589)

David knew that the walk with God was not an easy one, and would teach his disciples this very thing. It was well known that often, when someone new came to join one of his monasteries, David would leave them outside the front door and refuse to let them join the community until they were sure that God was calling them to it. He did this not out of spite or inhospitality, but from a complete understanding of Jesus' teaching that each person should weigh the cost of becoming a disciple (Luke 14:25–35).

On one occasion, David's monks were tested deeply by the behaviour of a group of women under the instruction of the wife of a man named Baia. This married couple had been displeased by the demonstrations of David's holiness and power, so one day Baia's wife took action.

> Inflamed with jealousy, [she] called her maids together and said, 'Go and deport yourselves with naked bodies in front of the monks, using crude words.' The maids obeyed, playing lewd games, imitating sexual intercourse, and displaying love's seductive embraces. They drew the minds of some of the monks toward desire… The monks sought to leave the place, but the holy father [David], steadfast with long-suffering patience and whose spirit could not be undermined or corrupted by riches, nor intimidated and exhausted by adversity, said to them, 'You know that the world hates you… The struggle is a clear sign of our own victory. For they who seek a promised heavenly homeland must be exhausted by adversities but not overcome and, with Christ as their ally… must overcome evil with good… Be strong therefore

and invincible in the struggle, in case your enemy should rejoice in your flight.' With these words he strengthened the resolve of his disciples.[48]

Meditation

Spend a few moments simply resting. Breathe gently and slowly. Become aware of the constant presence of God which envelops you and permeates you.

David knew that it is not an easy ride, living a life for God. He understood that each person must allow God to work within them to strengthen them so that they can resist temptation and hard times.

Today, it often seems that churches are so concerned with 'making converts' or 'getting people in' that there is little explanation of the hardships and temptations that each one will face when they step into a walk with Christ. Although the hand of God is there and divine power is at work, we are never promised that life will be easy as a Christian. Perhaps this teaching needs to be better understood and more widely shared among new disciples of Jesus, so that fewer will struggle with trials when they come.

What hardships are you facing at the moment? Which temptations defeat you most often? How might you allow God to work in you more, so that you can overcome the difficulties and stand against temptation more successfully?

Spend time with God now, dwelling upon these questions.

Scripture

Therefore let him who thinks he stands be careful that he doesn't fall. No temptation has taken you except what is common to man.

God is faithful, who will not allow you to be tempted above what you are able, but will with the temptation also make the way of escape, that you may be able to endure it. Therefore, my beloved, flee from idolatry. I speak as to wise men. Judge what I say.

1 CORINTHIANS 10:12–15

Blessing

May you remember that Christ is always with you, even through the hardest trials and battles.
May you be an influence on and example to those who come to you.
May you overcome all temptation that you face with God's strength working within you.

19
Finan

FEAST DAY: 17 February (d.661)

Finan became bishop of Lindisfarne when Aidan died, and he held the role for ten years. He built a wood-and-thatch church on Lindisfarne and continued the teaching style, rule and mission that Aidan had begun.

Finan saw the conversion to Christianity of Peada, the king of Mercia. Peada's father, Penda, was the pagan king who had tried to destroy the work of Aidan and the Christian kings of Northumbria. Finan was the bishop who consecrated and sent out the mission to Mercia (the Middle Angles), a mission that included Cedd.

An Irish bishop, Ronan, who had chosen to adopt the Roman dating of Easter, tried to bring Northumbria and Lindisfarne in line with it too. Although small pockets and a few groups within Northumbria changed, Finan, who held the most powerful Christian position in Northumbria, was so dedicated to the way of faith in which he had been brought up, and which he believed to be the truth, that he refused to accept the change simply to come in line with the Roman church's wishes.

Finan's heart for mission, as well as his tenacity in his belief, marked him out as a great man of faith and inner strength. His influence spread throughout England, not only through his own life and teaching, but also through those who had received his teaching and then went out on mission.

Finan was an inspiration to many; those who were taught by him and loved him aspired to be like him.

Meditation

Spend a few moments simply resting. Breathe gently and slowly. Become aware of the constant presence of God which envelops you and permeates you.

Finan had big shoes to fill, taking on the role of bishop of Lindisfarne after Aidan. Although he continued what Aidan had been doing, using Aidan's rule, Finan was a different person and allowed God to work through him as himself, not trying to be someone else.

Knowing the gifts of those whom he taught, Finan chose the best people to take on missions.

Who most inspires you in your Christian journey? How do you live out their inspiration without copying them? How do you allow God to work in you to allow his potential to be realised in you?

Spend time with God now, dwelling upon these questions.

Scripture

As for you, Titus, promote the kind of living that reflects wholesome teaching. Teach the older men to exercise self-control, to be worthy of respect, and to live wisely. They must have sound faith and be filled with love and patience.

Similarly, teach the older women to live in a way that honours God. They must not slander others or be heavy drinkers. Instead, they should teach others what is good. These older women must train the younger women to love their husbands and their children, to live wisely and be pure, to work in their homes, to do good, and to be submissive to their husbands. Then they will not bring shame on the word of God.

In the same way, encourage the young men to live wisely. And you yourself must be an example to them by doing good works of every kind. Let everything you do reflect the integrity and seriousness of your teaching. Teach the truth so that your teaching can't be criticised. Then those who oppose us will be ashamed and have nothing bad to say about us.

TITUS 2:1–8 (NLT)

Blessing

May you know the inspiration of great men and women of faith.
May you live your life as yourself, with their inspiration within you.
May the life you live be an inspiration to others.

20

Finbarr

FEAST DAY: 25 September (d.610)

Finbarr's father was an artisan and his mother was a lady of the Irish royal court. He was baptised 'Lochan' and educated at Kilmacahil in Kilkenny, where the monks named him 'Fionnbharr' ('the white head') because of his light-coloured hair. On one occasion, while returning from a pilgrimage to Rome, he visited David in Wales.

Finbarr travelled around southern Ireland, preaching and teaching, and then felt called to live as a hermit on a small island at Lough Eiroe. Like the Desert Fathers and Mothers who went out to live solitary lives, Finbarr was soon visited by others wanting to learn from him and experience the indwelling presence of God that surrounded and permeated him. Some of the visitors believed that this place would be their place of resurrection (where they would be born into glory), so Finbarr gave them the land as a gift.

He then went on to build a hermitage on the River Lee, where a similar thing happened: many folk came to visit him. Finbarr therefore founded a monastery that developed into the city of Cork, and the hermitage itself is thought to have become St Finbarr's Cathedral in the city.

Many wondrous miracles are attributed to Finbarr; they were seen throughout his life, but they began even before he was born. Finbarr's mother became pregnant by a man of high regard, but the king had also fallen in love with her. When the king discovered that she was pregnant with the other man's child, he grew enraged and sentenced them both to be burned to death at the stake. The driest wood was to be used, to ensure a swift and hot fire. The two were bound and set upon the wood. 'But divine power prevented [their being burned alive] for the elements obeyed God, resisting one another, lest that deed be accomplished. For the fire was, after a wonderful manner, extinguished… God did this on account of the holy infant who was enclosed in his mother's womb.'[49] In another version of the *Life of Finbarr* God caused a mighty rainstorm to fall just as they were about to light the fire, which prevented the burning. Supposedly, too, the sun did not set for two weeks after Finbarr died.

Meditation

Spend a few moments simply resting. Breathe gently and slowly. Become aware of the constant presence of God which envelops you and permeates you.

Finbarr desired to be a hermit but, because of the life he lived, many people wanted to come and learn from him. He was willing to set up monastic centres in the places where he went for solitude, because he believed that was God's will.

How willing are you to change your preferred course of action if it seems that God's will is different from yours? Are you willing to allow others to 'interfere' with what you are doing if God is leading their life path to intersect yours?

Spend time with God now, dwelling upon these questions.

Scripture

He came out, and went, as his custom was, to the Mount of Olives. His disciples also followed him. When he was at the place, he said to them, 'Pray that you don't enter into temptation.'

He was withdrawn from them about a stone's throw, and he knelt down and prayed, saying, 'Father, if you are willing, remove this cup from me. Nevertheless, not my will, but yours, be done.'

An angel from heaven appeared to him, strengthening him. Being in agony he prayed more earnestly. His sweat became like great drops of blood falling down on the ground.

LUKE 22:39–44

Blessing

May you know God's leading and guidance in your life.
May you recognise when God's will is different from yours.
May you be willing to change what you desire to do, if God's will is
   different from yours.

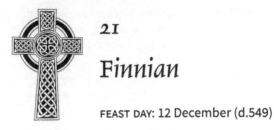

21

Finnian

FEAST DAY: 12 December (d.549)

Finnian travelled for years to both Britain and mainland Europe, dedicating himself to humble learning and instruction in the Christian faith. His travels included a time at St Martin's monastery in Tours. On his return to Ireland, he moved around, teaching and preaching what he had learned, and founding numerous churches and monastic centres, including the famous monastic centre of Skellig Michael. He was known as an enigmatic teacher, and many people would crowd to hear his expositions of scripture and biblical stories.

The final monastic centre that Finnian founded was in Clonard, where he eventually died and was buried. Finnian was led to Clonard by an angelic vision. Thousands of people at a time, including the famous 'twelve apostles of Ireland', came and learned from him there. The twelve apostles included Ciaran of Clonmacnoise, Brendan the Navigator and Columba of Iona.

Finnian's character and teaching, therefore, had a vast and deep influence on Celtic Christianity across much of Britain, Ireland and beyond. His is arguably the greatest, most long-lasting legacy, if you consider the consequent generations of Celtic Christian missionaries and the founding of monastic centres by those who were influenced either directly by Finnian or by his disciples.

Finnian's life was deeply dedicated to learning and teaching. His humble attitude towards his own learning, and his years of dedication to deepening his own faith before he shared his learning with others, proved to be extremely effective.

His God-given gift as an inspiring teacher and his closeness to God, through which he could be led by angels, meant that he stayed on the path by which God was leading him, and encouraged others to do the same. The 'ripple effect' of Finnian's life and teaching was wide and long-lasting.

Meditation

Spend a few moments simply resting. Breathe gently and slowly. Become aware of the constant presence of God which envelops you and permeates you.

Finnian understood that he must learn before he could teach. Because of his dedication to his own learning, and his dedication to following the divine leading, Finnian was arguably the most influential of all Celtic saints.

How do you view your learning on the spiritual path? Where do you learn best? How dedicated are you to following the divine guidance that flows through your life?

Spend time with God now, dwelling upon these questions.

Scripture

For every creature of God is good, and nothing is to be rejected, if it is received with thanksgiving. For it is sanctified through the word of God and prayer. If you instruct the brothers of these things, you will be a good servant of Christ Jesus, nourished in the words of the faith, and of the good doctrine which you have followed. But refuse profane and old wives' fables. Exercise yourself toward godliness. For bodily exercise has some value, but godliness has value in all things, having the promise of the life which is now, and of that which is to come. This saying is faithful and worthy of all acceptance. For to this end we both labour and suffer reproach, because we have set our trust in the living God, who is the Saviour of all men, especially of those who believe. Command and teach these things.

Let no man despise your youth; but be an example to those who believe, in word, in your way of life, in love, in spirit, in faith, and in purity. Until I come, pay attention to reading, to exhortation, and to teaching. Don't neglect the gift that is in you, which was given to you by prophecy, with the laying on of the hands of the elders. Be diligent in these things. Give yourself wholly to them, that your progress may be revealed to all. Pay attention to yourself, and to your teaching. Continue in these things, for in doing this you will save both yourself and those who hear you.

1 TIMOTHY 4:4–16

Blessing

May you be inspired by those who teach you.
May you know and follow the divine leading.
May you pass on what you have learned to others.

22
Gildas (the Wise)

FEAST DAY: 29 January (d.570)

After training in Illtyd's monastic college, along with David of Wales, Gildas could see much that was wrong in the mainstream church, so he became a hermit and moved to Somerset to write his most famous work, *De Excidio Britanniae* (*On the Ruin of Britain*—still available today). Much of our historical knowledge of his time comes from this book, and Bede quoted it and took it as a primary source for the beginning of his own *Ecclesiastical History of the English People. On the Ruin of Britain*, reflecting the Lamentations of Jeremiah in the Bible, chronicles the descent of the church in Britain from its original calling and mission to the 'mess' it was during Gildas' time, in the sixth century.

In *De Excidio Britanniae*, Gildas says that the Christian faith was brought to the shores of Britain in the latter part of the reign of Tiberius Caesar.[50] Tiberius reigned between AD14 and 37. Assuming, as most historians do, that the supposed changeover year between BC and AD is slightly adrift from the actual birth of Christ, which took place a few years earlier, this would mean that the Christian gospel reached Britain within ten years of Jesus' death. This is quite possible, as the trade routes between the Middle East and south-west Britain and southern Ireland are much older than that. Some people from the holy land who had accepted Christ, or converts from the missionary journeys of the apostle Paul, may well have come to Britain as traders a short time after the events described in Acts, bringing the teachings of Jesus and sharing their faith with local people.

Gildas includes various battles in his book, including the battle at Badon Hill, which was traditionally one of the greatest battles of King

Arthur. Gildas does not mention Arthur specifically: this is thought to be because, in legend, Arthur killed Gildas' brother, and so Gildas refused to name Arthur in his book.

Gildas ended his days in Brittany, in today's western France. He was very well known and sought after for his knowledge and wisdom. He taught many people who came to him when he was a hermit in Somerset and in Brittany.

Meditation

Spend a few moments simply resting. Breathe gently and slowly. Become aware of the constant presence of God which envelops you and permeates you.

Gildas desired an authentic and holy life and church. When he felt that the church was not authentic and holy, he wrote down his thoughts and, like the Old Testament prophets, presented them to God's people. He did this not simply to talk badly of the church or express his negativity towards it, but to expose the church's failings so that it might get back to its original calling and become holy and authentic again.

How do you react when you become despondent about the church? Do you simply talk badly of it 'behind its back', as it were? Is there a more productive way in which you could respond when the church you encounter does not seem to be fulfilling its purpose?

Spend time with God now, dwelling upon these questions.

Scripture

And to the angel of the assembly in Sardis write: He who has the seven Spirits of God, and the seven stars says these things:

'I know your works, that you have a reputation of being alive, but you are dead. Wake up, and keep the things that remain, which you were about to throw away, for I have found no works of yours perfected before my God. Remember therefore how you have received and heard. Keep it, and repent. If therefore you won't watch, I will come as a thief, and you won't know what hour I will come upon you. Nevertheless you have a few names in Sardis that did not defile their garments. They will walk with me in white, for they are worthy. He who overcomes will be arrayed in white garments, and I will in no way blot his name out of the book of life, and I will confess his name before my Father, and before his angels. He who has an ear, let him hear what the Spirit says to the assemblies.'

REVELATION 3:1–6

Blessing

*May you be like Gildas, seeing any wrong that takes place within
    churches and taking a positive stand to make it right.
May you not only gain knowledge, but also exercise wisdom.
May you know the power and peace that come from walking in
    authentic holiness with God.*

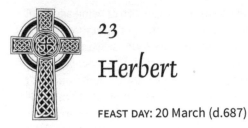

23
Herbert

FEAST DAY: 20 March (d.687)

Herbert was a hermit who lived on an island in the middle of the River Derwent. He was also an *anam chara* (soul friend) of Cuthbert of Lindisfarne for many years. Herbert would leave his hermitage every year to visit the busy Cuthbert and hear him teach, and the two were accustomed to sitting together for lengths of time, having discussions and 'refreshing each other with draughts of heavenly waters'.[51]

On one such visit, as they sat talking and encouraging one another in the Lord, Cuthbert suggested that if there was anything particular that Herbert wanted to discuss, now was the time. Cuthbert was convinced that God had spoken to him prophetically about his own future, and that this would be the two friends' last earthly meeting. 'I am certain,' he told Herbert, 'that the time of my departure and of laying aside my earthly tabernacle is at hand.'[52] The *anam chara* relationship of Herbert and Cuthbert was so close that, when Herbert heard this, he was distraught. With sighs and tears he begged Cuthbert to petition God that he would not be left without Cuthbert for a moment, but that 'as we served him together on earth, we may journey together… to behold his grace in heaven'.[53] Cuthbert prayed this while they were still together, then Herbert went back to his hermitage.

Just as Cuthbert's prophecy had said, he and Herbert did not see each other again in their earthly lives. Herbert suffered a terrible disease, and then at last Cuthbert's and Herbert's 'spirits left their bodies on one and the same day',[54] so that, just as Cuthbert had requested of God, his *anam chara* did not spend a moment of life on this earth without him.

Meditation

Spend a few moments simply resting. Breathe gently and slowly. Become aware of the constant presence of God which envelops you and permeates you.

The *anam chara* relationship was deeply loved by the Celts. A soul friend is a companion on the journey of life, with whom you can share all things—someone with whom you have a deep platonic relationship, so that you are able to be transparent with and encourage one another.

Do you have an *anam chara*? If so, how open and honest are you with them? If not, have you thought of finding one?[55]

Spend time with God now, dwelling upon these questions.

Scripture

As iron sharpens iron, so a friend sharpens a friend.
PROVERBS 27:17 (NLT)

Blessing

May you know the deep love and acceptance of an anam chara.
May you be blessed with a companion on the journey of life.
May you be willing to be vulnerable and available in this relationship.

24
Hilda

FEAST DAY: 17 November (d.680)

Hilda (or Hild) was born into the pagan Angle royal families of Northumberland and East Anglia. It was a time of war and insecure kingdoms, and she spent some time on the run or as a refugee in her own land. Once, along with her great-uncle, King Edwin of Northumbria, Hilda heard the Roman bishop Paulinus preach. She and Edwin were so taken with the story of Jesus that they committed their lives to following this new God, and Hilda was probably baptised by bishop Paulinus at York the following Easter. For the next almost 20 years, Hilda lived the life of a noblewoman in the royal court.

After the death of Edwin, Oswald, a young relative who had been sent to Iona during the wars, became king, and Aidan travelled from the Iona monastery to establish a monastic mission centre on Lindisfarne in Northumbria. Inspired by Aidan's life and expression of the Christian faith, which was so different from the Roman expression, and having built an *anam chara* relationship with him, Hilda began to live the Celtic way of Christian life. She felt that God was calling her to become a nun, and so she decided to join her sister, who was a nun at Chelles in Gaul (now France). However, Aidan sent a message to her, saying that he believed God wanted her to stay in Britain. (While Hilda was still in her mother's womb, her mother had had a vision of a necklace with a jewel that shone light across the whole of Britain. Bede believed this to have been a prophetic vision of the light of Christ shining from Hilda.)[56]

Hilda was given a small plot of land near the River Wear, where she made a hermitage. Later, Aidan made her abbess of a religious house at Hartlepool, which she ran in accordance with the traditional Celtic rule, like Lindisfarne and Iona. Finally, she founded a monastery for both men and women in Whitby.

Whitby soon became a centre for learning, where literature and the arts were encouraged as forms of worship. Work and trades were also fostered there. One of the workers in the monastery was the illiterate cowherd called Cædmon who became known as 'the Bard of Christ'.

Hilda, along with her friend Cuthbert, worked hard at trying to find a peaceful solution to the conflicts between the Celtic and Roman churches. In 664 Hilda offered her monastery as a venue for a synod to try to settle the matter once and for all. She spoke out for reconciliation and compromise on both sides, but Wilfrid argued so determinedly and persuasively for the Romanised structure that the king decided that the Celtic church must be brought in line with Roman structure and rule.

The Celtic delegates were bitterly disappointed. This, to them, was the end of the Celtic church and the traditions they loved so much. Hilda, however, accepted defeat gracefully and humbly. She brought her monasteries into line with the Romanised structure, changing to the rule of Benedict, even though she loved the Celtic expression.

Ten years later Hilda became unwell. She remained ill for six years until she died. Her last words to her devotees were, 'Keep the peace of the gospel with one another, and indeed with the entire world.'

Meditation

Spend a few moments simply resting. Breathe gently and slowly. Become aware of the constant presence of God which envelops you and permeates you.

Hilda had taken on the Christian teaching in one expression, but found, for her, a more life-giving expression of the faith in a different stream. She transformed the way in which she understood and expressed her faith, rather than simply remaining in the tradition she had known and practised for many years.

How willing are you to step out of your traditional way of doing things if you feel drawn to a new or different way? Are you more committed to tradition than to God? How do you know that you are following the Spirit of God as you grow and transform, rather than being swept off with some 'ear-tickling' unbiblical teaching?

Spend time with God now, dwelling upon these questions.

Scripture

Preach the word; be urgent in season and out of season; reprove, rebuke, and exhort, with all patience and teaching. For the time will come when they will not listen to the sound doctrine, but, having itching ears, will heap up for themselves teachers after their own lusts; and will turn away their ears from the truth, and turn aside to fables. But you be sober in all things, suffer hardship, do the work of an evangelist, and fulfil your ministry.

2 TIMOTHY 4:2–5

Blessing

Trade with the gifts God has given you.
Bend your minds to holy learning, that you may escape the fretting moth of littleness of mind that would wear out your souls.
Brace your wills to action, that they may not be the spoils of weak desires.
Train your hearts and lips to song which gives courage to the soul.
Be buffeted by trials; learn to laugh.
Be reproved; give thanks.
Having failed, determine to succeed.
Anon, based on the teachings of Hilda of Whitby[57]

25
Illtyd

FEAST DAY: 6 November (d. early sixth century)

Illtyd (pronounced with the Welsh 'LL', not an English double 'L') was first a soldier and, so the legend says, fought alongside King Arthur. One day, when Illtyd and his men were out with a royal hunting party, the men came across a hermit called Cadoc and treated him terribly, but Cadoc refused to rise to retaliation. Illtyd saw this and was amazed. That night God spoke to him about the spiritual battle in which Cadoc was a great warrior. The following morning, Illtyd left his military life and went to seek out Cadoc, to live as a hermit and serve in the army of Christ, in which he fought valiantly within the spiritual realms.

As a hermit, Illtyd had a strong relationship with creation, especially the woodland creatures. He founded a monastic centre in Wales and is often seen as the founder of the Welsh church. His monasteries taught such people as David of Wales, Gildas the historian and Samson of Dol.

Illtyd's method was a holistic one, bringing harmony to mind, body and soul. He was known as a most learned man in the teachings of the Old and New Testaments, but also in philosophy, poetry, rhetoric, grammar and literature.

Illtyd was an inspiration for generations to come, and is still such today.

Meditation

Spend a few moments simply resting. Breathe gently and slowly. Become aware of the constant presence of God which envelops you and permeates you.

The Celtic understanding was that everything is one, with no separation between physical and spiritual, sacred and secular; there was no dualistic thinking. Our mind, body and soul, along with our spirit, are all parts of one whole person, and each person is a part of one whole creation, all belonging to and loved by God. Illtyd's method reflected this holistic understanding.

How do you understand your 'self'? Do you have a dualistic understanding of the world? Do you separate the sacred from the secular? Why do you think the Celts didn't do this? How do you think a non-dualistic view might help you in your life and create a better world?

Spend time with God now, dwelling upon these questions.

Scripture

One of the scribes came, and heard them questioning together. Knowing that he had answered them well, [he] asked him, 'Which commandment is the greatest of all?'

Jesus answered, 'The greatest is, "Hear, Israel, the Lord our God, the Lord is one: you shall love the Lord your God with all your heart, and with all your soul, and with all your mind, and with all your strength." This is the first commandment. The second is like this, "You shall love your neighbour as yourself." There is no other commandment greater than these.'

The scribe said to him, 'Truly, teacher, you have said well that he is one, and there is none other but he, and to love him with all the heart, and with all the understanding, with all the soul, and with all the strength, and to love his neighbour as himself, is more important than all whole burnt offerings and sacrifices.'

When Jesus saw that he answered wisely, he said to him, 'You are not far from God's Kingdom.'

No one dared ask him any question after that.

MARK 12:28–34

Blessing

May you know the spiritual battle to which you are called, and fight valiantly.
May you care for each individual, and yourself, as a whole person, not seeing anyone as just a 'soul to be saved'.
May you love the Lord your God with all your heart, and with all your soul, and with all your mind, and with all your strength.

26
John Scotus Eriugena

FEAST DAY: Unknown (d.877)

John Scotus Eriugena was a renowned theologian and scholar, whose name means something like 'John, the Scot of Ireland'. He brought the Christian mystic tradition firmly into Celtic Christianity, not only by his own teachings but also by translating the complete works of the fifth- or sixth-century Greek Christian mystic Dionysius the Areopagite (more commonly known today as Pseudo-Dionysius) and by writing a commentary on *Celestial Hierarchy*, part of the works of Pseudo-Dionysius.

Eriugena was theologian-in-residence to the Holy Roman Emperor King Charles the Bald, who was the grandson of Charlemagne. Eriugena wrote a wonderful homily on the prologue to the Gospel of John (that is, John 1:1–17), but perhaps most famous is his work *Periphyseon* or *On the Division of Nature*, in which he 'presents an understanding of the origin and meaning of the universe... [which] establishes the created world, both visible and invisible, as a theophany of God, who is unknowable in himself. God is thus simultaneously present in all things and infinitely beyond all things'.[58] The sense of the connectedness of humanity and nature, and of the ability to see and experience God within creation, is deeply woven into the teachings of Celtic Christianity, and nowhere more explicitly does it appear than in Eriugena's work.

Other Celtic saints also lead us to see God in creation, or to get to know the Creator through getting to know creation, but Eriugena draws us into a more mystical understanding of encounter with God in and through the natural world. As 'the Divine Essence can be grasped by no intellectual creature',[59] nature itself is a way in which we can encounter the unknowable (or 'ineffable') God. In Eriugena's *Homily on the Prologue of John's Gospel*, he states that we can 'learn to know the Maker from those things that are made in him and by him'.[60] According to Eriugena, then, through the creation an understanding of God can be gained. Eriugena believed that God is eternally creating, and that God's being and God's creating are one interwoven reality; God's being is in every part of what God has created. 'When we hear, then, that God makes all things, we should simply understand that God is in all things… He alone by himself truly has being… Those things with being [the natural world]… receive being by participation in him who, by himself, alone truly has being.'[61]

A subtle but significant distinction needs to be made here between nature gods and God in nature. The pagans and druids who populated Britain and Ireland both before the Roman armies arrived in Britain and, in a resurgence, after they left, were pantheistic—that is, they believed that nature is identical with divinity. Celtic Christians such as Eriugena, however, were panentheistic—that is, they believed that God is in every aspect of nature.

Meditation

Spend a few moments simply resting. Breathe gently and slowly. Become aware of the constant presence of God which envelops you and permeates you.

John Scotus Eriugena was a highly intelligent person who dwelt in the mystery of knowing the unknowable God. He saw all of creation as one great expression of God's being, and believed that people could encounter and see God within all of creation.

How do you view the natural world around you? Is it something that is just there, perhaps for you to use? Or do you see it as something more? If you see it as something more, something connected to God, does or should that change the way you act towards it and interact with it?

Spend time with God now, dwelling upon these questions.

Scripture

The basic reality of God is plain enough. Open your eyes and there it is! By taking a long and thoughtful look at what God has created, people have always been able to see what their eyes as such can't see: eternal power, for instance, and the mystery of his divine being. So nobody has a good excuse. What happened was this: people knew God perfectly well, but when they didn't treat him like God, refusing to worship him, they trivialised themselves into silliness and confusion so that there was neither sense nor direction left in their lives. They pretended to know it all, but were illiterate regarding life. They traded the glory of God who holds the whole world in his hands for cheap figurines you can buy at any roadside stand.

ROMANS 1:20–23 (*THE MESSAGE*)

Blessing

May you know the intelligence that God has given you, and use it well.
May you know God through creation and see God in all the world around you.
May you experience the mystical reality of knowing the unknowable God.

27
Kenneth

FEAST DAY: 11 October (d.600)

Kenneth (sometimes Canice or Cainneach) was an Irish Pict, renowned as a man of eloquence and learning, which is quite fitting for the son of an Irish bard and professional itinerant poet. He was one of the twelve apostles of Ireland from Finnian's monastery in Clonard, but he also studied under Cadoc in Wales. He wrote a commentary on the Gospels, which was referred to until the later Middle Ages.

Kenneth was a friend of Columba and travelled to Iona after Columba had established the monastic centre there. Columba had a prophecy of a 'certain man, holy and chosen, who will come to us before evening'.[62] Even though the sea was perilous and stormy that day, Kenneth had a smooth crossing and Columba received him the same evening with all honour and hospitality. He accompanied Columba on the first major mission from Iona to King Brude of the northern Picts. The mission took them all the way to the northernmost edge of Loch Ness, where Brude had his fort.

On this mission, which was met with hostility and barred gates on the king's fort, the king's druids, including the chief, Broichan, 'did all they could to prevent' it.[63] Eventually, however, the Christian message was received, and 'those whom the legions of the Caesars could not subdue by the sword were brought under the yoke of Christ by these few dauntless, unarmed missionaries'.[64]

Kenneth also travelled on his own missions both in Ireland and to the Picts. He founded churches and monastic centres throughout his missions, including one at Aghaboe, which sent missionaries to places as far away as Austria. One place that still bears his name is Kilkenny in Ireland (Cill Chainnigh, 'The church of Kenneth'). Kilkenny was one of the last parts of Ireland to be converted to Christianity. Tradition has it that Kenneth led a Christian force there to eliminate the last bastion of druidic rule in Ireland. The last archdruid of Ireland had retired with his council to Kilkenny for safety. Kenneth overcame their opposition, founding a Christian centre there. When he died, his body was placed in the Abbey of Aghaboe.

Meditation

Spend a few moments simply resting. Breathe gently and slowly. Become aware of the constant presence of God which envelops you and permeates you.

Kenneth spent time as a missionary with people of another belief. He withstood the opposition that they gave, and persevered with the gospel message. The spiritual power that flowed through Kenneth overcame the druids and the message of Christ was received.

How do you reach out to people of other faiths? Do you gently persevere at sharing the gospel of Christ with them, or are you daunted and afraid of any opposition that you might face? How might you share your faith with them?

Spend time with God now, dwelling upon these questions.

Scripture

Jesus came to them and spoke to them, saying, 'All authority has been given to me in heaven and on earth. Go, and make disciples of all nations, baptising them in the name of the Father and of the Son and of the Holy Spirit, teaching them to observe all things

that I commanded you. Behold, I am with you always, even to the
end of the age.' Amen.
MATTHEW 28:18–20

Blessing

May you know the leading of God to share the message of your faith.
May you encounter people with different beliefs from your own.
May you persevere, gently, through opposition, sharing the gospel
*   with love.*

28

Kentigern (or Mungo)

FEAST DAY: 13 January (d.612)

Kentigern was almost not born. A child conceived due to the rape of his mother Tannoc, his fate lay in what would happen to his mother. When Tannoc's father, the local chieftain, found out she was pregnant by rape, and therefore disgraced, he had her thrown off a cliff, an alternative punishment to stoning. But mother and baby survived the fall, so her father ordered his soldiers to put Tannoc in a small boat with no oars, no rudder and no sail, and push her out into the North Sea to starve or drown. After the boat had floated on the open sea for a time, the tides brought it safely to the shores at Culross, where Tannoc was taken in by the monks. When the child was born, Tannoc named him Kentigern, which means 'Big chief', possibly a sarcastic slight on her father and his attempts to kill them both. The head monk at Culross, however, gave him the affectionate nickname Mungo, which means literally 'my dog' but may also be understood as 'my beloved'.

When Kentigern was small, he was out with some boys when a stone thrown by one of them hit a robin on the head and knocked it to the ground. Kentigern held the robin in his hand and prayed for its recovery. Instantly the bird jumped up and flew off. The robin is still pictured in the coat of arms of the city of Glasgow, which Kentigern is reputed to have founded.

Later in life, Kentigern founded many monasteries and changed many people's lives. One of the stories from Kentigern's life is related to part of the Arthurian legend. One day in the forests of Celidon, near Clyde, Kentigern was praying when a half-naked, crazed man came running towards him. Unfazed, Kentigern spoke calmly with the man and found out that he was in the woods as a self-punishment for causing a battle in which many people had lost their lives. He had come to believe in the Christian God and that his punishment was God's will. The man, named Lailoken (pronounced 'Ly-lo-kin'), also known as Merlin, was blessed by Kentigern. His temperament instantly calmed, and although he stayed in the forest for some time, prophesying (as he was a seer), he became more and more reconciled with God and at peace within himself. At last he was able to reconnect with society in his previous position. In remembrance of this legend, a stained-glass window of Kentigern with Merlin can be found in Stobo Kirk, Peeblesshire, Scotland.

Before his death, Kentigern met with Columba and the two powerful men of God shared time with God together.

Meditation

Spend a few moments simply resting. Breathe gently and slowly. Become aware of the constant presence of God which envelops you and permeates you.

Kentigern seemed to have the hand of God upon him from before he was born. Throughout his life, he followed the touch and movement of this hand, and shared it with everyone, from half-crazed wild men in the woods to holy monks who led significant monastic centres and taught many people.

How do you understand the hand of God upon your life? Do you believe that God has had his hand upon you since before you were born, and has plans for you?

Spend time with God now, dwelling upon these questions.

Scripture

Yahweh, you have searched me,
and you know me.
You know my sitting down and my rising up.
You perceive my thoughts from afar.
You search out my path and my lying down,
and are acquainted with all my ways.
For there is not a word on my tongue,
but, behold, Yahweh, you know it altogether.
You hem me in behind and before.
You laid your hand on me.
This knowledge is beyond me.
It's lofty.
I can't attain it.
Where could I go from your Spirit?
Or where could I flee from your presence?
If I ascend up into heaven, you are there.
If I make my bed in Sheol, behold, you are there!
If I take the wings of the dawn,
and settle in the uttermost parts of the sea;
Even there your hand will lead me,
and your right hand will hold me.
If I say, 'Surely the darkness will overwhelm me;
the light around me will be night';
even the darkness doesn't hide from you,
but the night shines as the day.
The darkness is like light to you.
For you formed my inmost being.
You knit me together in my mother's womb.
I will give thanks to you,
for I am fearfully and wonderfully made.
Your works are wonderful.
My soul knows that very well.

My frame wasn't hidden from you,
when I was made in secret,
woven together in the depths of the earth.
Your eyes saw my body.
In your book they were all written,
the days that were ordained for me,
when as yet there were none of them.
How precious to me are your thoughts, God!
How vast is their sum!
If I would count them, they are more in number than the sand.
When I wake up, I am still with you.

PSALM 139:1–18

Blessing

May you know that, no matter what the circumstances, God is in
control and has a great plan.
May you be a friend to the earth and to those who are outcast within
it, speaking the calm love of God into their lives.
May you walk the path that God lays before you and be a great
influence in the world for the good of God's kingdom.

29

Kevin

FEAST DAY: 3 June (d.618)

Born to nobles, educated by monks and living as a hermit, Kevin was one of those people whom others are just drawn to. He settled as a hermit by the upper lake at Glendalough (pronounced 'glen-da-lokh'), meaning 'glen of two lakes', in Ireland. But as people kept being drawn to this man, many staying close by, the place soon became too small, so they moved with Kevin to the larger area of the lower lake, where the best-preserved Celtic community of God still remains.

The problem was that the lower lake was said to be the home of a 'great fearsome monster'. Legend says that Kevin tamed the great monster with the peace and power of God. He went and stood in the lower lake to pray. The monster came up to attack Kevin by wrapping itself around him, but Kevin continued to pray. The monster, instead of crushing him, simply remained there in peace, surrounding him. Kevin then got the monster to move from the lower lake into the upper lake, away from the community but near to where he himself stayed. He tamed the beast and lived with it.

Kevin was a man of deep prayer and intimate love of God. He would spend a great deal of time in peace at prayer—once, long enough for a blackbird to nest in his hand, which was stretched out of the window of his cell during a 'cross' vigil. He would then teach others what he had learned.

Meditation

Spend a few moments simply resting. Breathe gently and slowly. Become aware of the constant presence of God which envelops you and permeates you.

Kevin was a man of deep inner peace. The greatest lesson passed down from him comes from his taming of the monster—a metaphor for the taming of our inner 'monsters' by peace, prayer and the power of God. Rather than getting rid of the inner monster, we are able to live with it once it has been tamed through inner peace, acceptance and prayer by the movement of God's power within us.

What are your 'inner monsters'—the things with which you battle? Have you been trying, and failing, to get rid of an inner beast? What if, with the peace and power of God, through prayer, you were able to subdue the monster and, instead of getting rid of it, live with it as something tamed? (We might understand this as similar to Dr Carl Jung's ideas about 'owning your shadow side'.)

Spend time with God now, dwelling upon these questions.

Scripture

In nothing be anxious, but in everything, by prayer and petition with thanksgiving, let your requests be made known to God. And the peace of God, which surpasses all understanding, will guard your hearts and your thoughts in Christ Jesus.

Finally, brothers, whatever things are true, whatever things are honourable, whatever things are just, whatever things are pure, whatever things are lovely, whatever things are of good report; if there is any virtue, and if there is any praise, think about these things.

PHILIPPIANS 4:6–8

Blessing

*May you have such a presence of God within you that it simply draws
people to you and, consequently, to Christ.
May you know the peace and strength of the Creator God within you.
May you be still in that peace and strength and, through prayer, still
and tame your inner 'monsters'.*

30
Melangell

FEAST DAY: 27 May (d.590)

Melangell was a beautiful Irish princess who escaped to Wales when her father arranged a marriage for her with a great Irishman. Melangell desired to remain a holy virgin for God, so she fled, being led by God across the sea. She found a secluded valley in Wales, where she stayed for 15 years as a hermit before she saw another human face. The human face she then saw was that of Prince Brychwel Ysgithrog, who owned the land upon which she had been residing.

The prince was out on a hunt with his hounds and was chasing a hare which had run into a thorny thicket. Brychwel and the dogs went through the thicket to get the hare, but when they found it, it was resting under the edges of a lady's garments. Brychwel urged his dogs on to catch the hare, but 'the more he shouted, urging them on, the further the dogs retreated and, howling, fled from the little animal Finally the prince, altogether astonished, asked the girl how long she had lived on her own in these lands… [and] who she was, her place of birth and origins.'[65] Melangell told the prince everything.

On hearing Melangell's story, Prince Brychwel, a Christian himself, was cut to the heart and offered the lands upon which Melangell had spent the past 15 years 'for the service of God, that they may be a perpetual asylum, refuge, and defence… Let neither king nor prince seek to be so rash or bold toward God that they presume to drag away any man or woman who has escaped here.'[66] Melangell continued in the same place as a hermit for 37 years, giving shelter and refuge not only to men and women, to whom she also taught the ways of a hermit of God, but also to all manner of animals. No matter what type they were, or how wild, when entering the place or the presence of Melangell herself they became calm and non-violent, as if they had been tame or domesticated animals. 'Nor, by the aid of Divine mercy, were miracles and various other signs lacking for those who called upon her help and the grace and favour with an inner motion of the heart.'[67]

Meditation

Spend a few moments simply resting. Breathe gently and slowly. Become aware of the constant presence of God which envelops you and permeates you.

Melangell was a woman of such deep peace and the indwelling presence of God that everyone and everything that came to her rested in that peace. Through this embodiment of divine peace, Melangell expressed deep hospitality.

How do you embody the peace of God? How do others perceive this peace? Does it dwell within you? What might you do to enhance both your awareness of divine peace and others' awareness of peace dwelling within you? How might you express this peace through hospitality?

Spend time with God now, dwelling upon these questions.

Scripture

Let love be without hypocrisy. Abhor that which is evil. Cling to that which is good. In love of the brothers be tenderly affectionate to one another; in honour preferring one another; not lagging in diligence; fervent in spirit; serving the Lord; rejoicing in hope; enduring in troubles; continuing steadfastly in prayer; contributing to the needs of the saints; given to hospitality. Bless those who persecute you; bless, and don't curse. Rejoice with those who rejoice. Weep with those who weep. Be of the same mind one toward another. Don't set your mind on high things, but associate with the humble. Don't be wise in your own conceits. Repay no one evil for evil. Respect what is honourable in the sight of all men. If it is possible, as much as it is up to you, be at peace with all men.

ROMANS 12:9-18

Blessing

May you know the deep peace of the Prince of Peace.
May that peace flow through you into the lives of others.
May you express that peace through hospitality, without prejudice,
    to all.

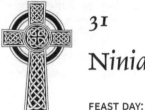

31
Ninian

FEAST DAY: 16 September (d.432)

Ninian lived at the time of the Romans' departure from Britain. He was keen to keep his Christian faith alive, so he went to mainland Europe to learn and gain spiritual maturity and strength. He spent some time in Tours, being taught by Martin. Martin had learned the Christian faith of the Desert Fathers and Mothers, who had left the main cities and set up hermitages in the desert. These desert-dwellers had soon been joined by others seeking spiritual direction from them rather than staying with the commercialised, sanitised Christian faith of the Roman Empire in the cities.

Ninian took this teaching back to his home in what is now Scotland and set up the first officially recognised community of God for the service and worship of Christ, known as *Candida Casa*, or 'The White/Shining House'. This was a whole new concept and a totally fresh expression of the Christian faith.

Ninian stood out as someone different, someone holy, someone 'more'. This drew many people to want to know about Christ.

Ninian is the first recorded person to use the 'Caim' prayer. 'Caim' is a Celtic word meaning 'to encircle' and it denoted protection. Caim prayers became well used in the Celtic church, and many of those who follow the way of Celtic Christian spirituality today use them as encircling prayers of protection.

Ninian was once asked by a farmer to help him protect his cattle from marauders who had been travelling the nearby countryside. Ninian, despite the objections of the farmer, took the cattle into the middle of the field. He stood them together and began to walk sun-wise around them, dragging his staff along the ground to create a circle in the earth. As he walked, he prayed a Caim prayer of protection. Then he went into the farmer's house to sleep for the night.

Sure enough, that night, the marauders came to that very field. Seeing the cattle just standing there, they went to take them—an easy steal, so they thought. But as each of them crossed the line that Ninian had drawn, they collapsed in agony. The chief of the band caught his side on a cow's horn as he fell, causing his intestines to spill out. The marauders managed to crawl out of the circle and drag their leader to the edge of the field. Ninian came out of the farmer's house and went to the injured man. Placing the intestines back inside him, Ninian prayed for healing, and the cut that had been caused by the horn of the cow healed completely. The men were both terrified and amazed. They listened to Ninian speak of the power of Christ.

Many miraculous stories surround the life of Ninian, and his style of teaching encouraged his disciples to experience the kingdom of God fully lived in everyday life. Supernatural power flowed through him, and even through his staff, when it was stolen once. There were no half-measures of faith with Ninian.

Meditation

Spend a few moments simply resting. Breathe gently and slowly. Become aware of the constant presence of God which envelops you and permeates you.

Ninian was someone of great faith and total obedience to God. He had complete faith in the power of God to work on earth, and he believed that God's kingdom was active here on earth. He did not simply speak about this belief but acted it out, and consequently saw the fullness of God's power move through him and in his life.

How do you understand the power of God working in your life? In what ways have you experienced it? Do you believe that you can work in this power today?

Spend time with God now, dwelling upon these questions.

Scripture

But you will receive power when the Holy Spirit has come upon you. You will be witnesses to me in Jerusalem, in all Judea and Samaria, and to the uttermost parts of the earth.
ACTS 1:8

'Most certainly I tell you, he who believes in me, the works that I do, he will do also; and he will do greater works than these, because I am going to my Father.'
JOHN 14:12

Blessing

May you be someone who commits totally to your faith.
May you be someone who gives no half-hearted effort in your walk,
*   but lives life fully committed to God.*
May you be an example of Christ to the people you meet.

32
Oswald

FEAST DAY: 5 August (d.642)

Oswald became king of Northumbria following the death of Edwin. Oswald had been sent, along with the other young children of Edwin's royal family, to the monastic centre on Iona to be kept safe during the inter-kingdom wars, so he had been brought up on Iona, gaining training and wisdom in the Christian faith in the Celtic tradition. Edwin had been a Christian in the Roman tradition, and, following the custom of the day, the people of the kingdom followed his beliefs. However, after his death at the hand of the pagan King Penda, the people reverted to their pagan past, perhaps anticipating Penda's rule or just because they were not really Christians.

Oswald, 'the most Christian king of Northumbria',[68] then won the throne from Penda through battle. After setting up a cross on the battlefield (now known as Heavenfield), he wanted the people of his new kingdom to know the reality and grace and power of the Christian God, which he had grown to know and experience on Iona. He sent for some monks to come from Iona and start a mission in Northumbria. The first attempt failed and the group went back to Iona reporting that the Northumbrian people were 'intractable, obstinate, and uncivilised'.[69] After a meeting, a second mission was arranged, with the newly appointed bishop Aidan leading the group. Aidan was a much gentler man, but not lacking in zeal.

Oswald granted Aidan land, anywhere he would like, to place his monastic and mission centre, and Aidan chose Lindisfarne. Oswald travelled with Aidan on his missions, working as his translator while Aidan learned the dialect of the Northumbrian Angles. This humility was well noted; Oswald won a great deal of respect from his people, and his kingdom grew in influence right across the land.

> Oswald gained from the one God who made heaven and earth greater earthly realms than any of his ancestors had possessed; in fact he held under his sway all the peoples and kingdoms of Britain, divided among the speakers of four different languages, British, Pictish, Irish, and English. Though he wielded supreme power over the whole land, he was always wonderfully humble, kind and generous to the poor and to strangers.[70]

Meditation

Spend a few moments simply resting. Breathe gently and slowly. Become aware of the constant presence of God which envelops you and permeates you.

Oswald, 'the saintly and victorious king of the Northumbrians',[71] was the epitome of a humble servant-king. He held his position and power lightly and was willing to take on lowly positions, such as travelling interpreter, for the sake of the kingdom of God.

What are you willing to give up for the sake of the kingdom of God? Are you willing to take on lowly roles which might be 'beneath you', if needs be? What does it mean to be humble?

Spend time with God now, dwelling upon these questions.

Scripture

> [Jesus] came to Capernaum, and when he was in the house he asked them, 'What were you arguing among yourselves on the way?'

But they were silent, for they had disputed one with another on the way about who was the greatest.

He sat down, and called the twelve; and he said to them, 'If any man wants to be first, he shall be last of all, and servant of all.'
MARK 9:33–35

Blessing

May you know the divine calling upon your life.
May you take up the positions to which God calls you .
May you be willing to be humble in order to raise God to the highest place.

33
Patrick

FEAST DAY: 17 March (d.461)

Patrick probably grew up on the north-west coast of Britain, in an area known as Rheged. He was from a Christian family of noble birth, but was a wild youth. At 16 he was kidnapped by pirate raiders from Ireland and taken back and sold there as a slave. Patrick, although he was not a Christian himself at this point, later recalls that his kidnapping was 'because [he] departed from God, and kept not his precepts, and [was] not obedient to the priests who admonished us for our salvation'.[72] His work as a slave was to care for animals on the Irish hills. There he found his own relationship with God, which grew deep indeed and included many mystical encounters with the divine. He became a man of deep prayer, praying, so he said, over 100 prayers during the day, and a similar number at night.

Patrick was a man of dreams and visions and ecstatic spiritual experiences, and in one of these he saw a boat which would allow him freedom from his slavery. So, when opportunity arose, he escaped and travelled the coast of Ireland for over 200 miles until he found the boat that he had seen in his vision. At first he was not allowed on board, but eventually he got passage. During the trip (which was probably to northern France), a great storm came upon the ship. All on board feared they would drown, until Patrick spoke of Christ who could calm the waves. After telling the story from the Bible, Patrick stood on the deck of the boat and prayed. The storm and the great waves settled down and the sea became calm.

Eventually Patrick found his way back to north-west Britain, to his family home, where he was implored never to leave again. But soon after this, in another vision, he saw a man come to him with a letter. It was the voice of the Irish people, pleading for him to come back to tell them about Christ. This he did, and the result was perhaps one of the most famous Christian missions in British and Irish ecclesiastical history.

Stories abound about Patrick's time in Ireland, from the famous Easter fire near Tara hill to the appearance of a group of deer that allowed Patrick and a few disciples to escape some pursuing soldiers, to the driving out of all snakes from the land of Ireland. This last story may refer to Patrick's confrontations with the druids, who often used the sign of a snake. Rather than being about literal snakes, it may be related to the rise of Christianity and the decline of the druidic religion across Ireland, throughout, and following, Patrick's life and mission.

Meditation

Spend a few moments simply resting. Breathe gently and slowly. Become aware of the constant presence of God which envelops you and permeates you.

Patrick had visions and ecstatic mystical experiences of the divine. What are your experiences of the mystical and ecstatic side of your relationship with God? How might you be able to encounter God in this way more? Patrick spent a great deal of time in prayer and dwelling in the divine presence, thus creating the inner environment to encounter God. How might you improve your 'dwelling time' with God?

Spend time with God now, dwelling upon these questions.

Scripture

It is doubtless not profitable for me to boast. For I will come to visions and revelations of the Lord. I know a man in Christ, fourteen years ago (whether in the body, I don't know, or whether out of the body, I don't know; God knows), such a one caught up into the third heaven. I know such a man (whether in the body, or outside of the body, I don't know; God knows), how he was caught up into Paradise, and heard unspeakable words, which it is not lawful for a man to utter. On behalf of such a one I will boast, but on my own behalf I will not boast, except in my weaknesses. For if I would desire to boast, I will not be foolish; for I will speak the truth. But I refrain, so that no man may think more of me than that which he sees in me, or hears from me.

2 CORINTHIANS 12:1–6

Blessing

May you spend time dwelling with God, creating the inner
environment to experience the divine.
May you be open to the movement of God's Spirit within you, drawing
you into the mystical and ecstatic.
May you not boast of these experiences, but use them to help others
grow closer to God.

34
Pelagius

FEAST DAY: Unknown (d.418)

Pelagius is arguably the most controversial figure in Celtic Christianity. Most probably a British Celt, his writings express the 'deeply communitarian and ascetical values of the early monasticism that flourished throughout the Celtic Lands'.[73] In around AD380, Pelagius appeared in Rome, where he stayed for almost 30 years as a well-respected theologian until around 409.

> Pelagius was the spiritual advisor to many Christians in Rome, and in fact moved about successfully in the Roman Christian circles of Jerome. In Rome Pelagius emerged as a theologian to be reckoned with and as a man who had great personal sanctity, moral fervour and charisma… Pelagius was evidently a major religious intellectual force of his time. He always made a point of showing that his ideas had a solid basis in the writings of the Church Fathers. At least until 415 Pelagius was widely accepted as an orthodox Christian theologian.[74]

In 409, Pelagius, along with many others, was driven out of Rome by the imminent attack of the Visigoths. Over the next few years he and his pupil Celestius opposed some of the teachings and doctrines of the Church of Rome, and Augustine in particular—especially Augustine's belief in predestination, and the doctrine of original sin. It is probable that Pelagius wasn't just a lone voice opposing Rome, but the chosen voice of the Christian people in Celtic Britain to challenge the Roman teaching.

Pelagius believed that human beings have free choice and are able to bring themselves to a place where they can gain salvation from God. This was misrepresented by Augustine as a statement that humans can bring themselves to salvation. Pelagius also believed that the very essence of humanity is the divine image and that everyone is made in the image of God, as Genesis says. The doctrine of original sin, however, states that the very essence of humanity is evil, ever since the fall in the garden of Eden; it goes on to say that without God no one has the capacity to do good, nor can anyone be held responsible for any evil actions they take. Pelagius opposed this teaching and said that everyone is responsible for their own actions.

Pelagius also wrote pastoral, apostolic-type letters, guiding his disciples in how to live more like Christ. In one letter he speaks very strongly against those who call themselves 'Christian' but do not act like Christ.[75] '[M]uch of what Pelagius argued in his ascetical rather than theological writings can be understood as the cry of indignation of an uncompromising rural monastic at the fashionable Christianity of Rome during the onset of a new and liberal age.'[76]

More than once, Augustine of Hippo took Pelagius' ideas and writings to Pope Innocent I and a church council, to try to get Pelagius condemned for heresy, but each time they judged that there was not enough in Pelagius' writings to warrant classing him as a heretic. Although he was not cleared of heresy, the verdict was 'undecided'. When Pope Innocent I was succeeded by Pope Zosimus, Augustine again attempted to get Pelagius condemned as a heretic. This time there was added pressure from the Roman Emperor Honorius to do so. Relenting to the pressure from the Emperor, Zosimus declared Pelagius a heretic and excommunicated him from Rome.

After the death of Pelagius, a following grew from some of his teachings. The cult of Pelagianism began, which expanded on Pelagius' thoughts, beyond what Pelagius himself had said and did. Indeed, this became a heretical belief, which Patrick confronted. It is important not to confuse what Pelagius said when he was alive with the teachings of Pelagianism that grew in popularity after his death.

Meditation

Spend a few moments simply resting. Breathe gently and slowly. Become aware of the constant presence of God which envelops you and permeates you.

Pelagius believed that each person who declares themselves a Christian should act like one. He had the courage to challenge those in authority when he felt that they were not teaching according to scripture.

How might you be sure that the way you are, and what you believe, are in alignment with the scriptures? How might others know that you are living a holy, godly, Christ-like life?

Spend time with God now, dwelling upon these questions.

Scripture

'Beware of false prophets, who come to you in sheep's clothing, but inwardly are ravening wolves. By their fruits you will know them. Do you gather grapes from thorns, or figs from thistles? Even so, every good tree produces good fruit; but the corrupt tree produces evil fruit. A good tree can't produce evil fruit, neither can a corrupt tree produce good fruit. Every tree that doesn't grow good fruit is cut down, and thrown into the fire. Therefore by their fruits you will know them. Not everyone who says to me, "Lord, Lord," will enter into the Kingdom of Heaven; but he who does the will of my Father who is in heaven. Many will tell me in that day, "Lord, Lord, didn't we prophesy in your name, in your name cast out demons, and in your name do many mighty

works?" Then I will tell them, "I never knew you. Depart from me, you who work iniquity."'
MATTHEW 7:15–23

Blessing

May the life you live be a godly, Christ-like one.
May you be transformed daily to become more like Christ.
May those around you know and witness this transformation by your 'fruits'.

35
Petroc

FEAST DAY: 4 June (d.564)

A British prince and modern patron saint of Cornwall, Petroc was probably born in south Wales. The earliest *Life* of Petroc states that he was the son of an unnamed Welsh king; the twelfth-century version known as the *Gotha Life*, written at Bodmin, identifies that king as Glywys of Glywysing. He ministered primarily to the Britons of Devon and Cornwall. He is associated with a monastery at Padstow, which is named after him (Pedroc-stowe, or 'Petroc's place').

Petroc studied in Ireland, where he is said, later, to have been the teacher of Kevin of Glendalough. He made a pilgrimage to Rome and, on returning to Cornwall, shut himself up in the monastery he founded at Padstow, standing at the mouth of the River Camel on the north Cornish coast. All accounts indicate that Petroc retired from Padstow to Bodmin, a vast moor in Cornwall, and there founded a second monastery and a great church. Petroc also founded churches in Little Petherick and Bodmin and in many parts of Britain, Wales and Brittany.

On one occasion when he was in Cornwall, where King Constantine ruled (not Constantine the Great, Emperor of Rome), Petroc saved a deer that Constantine was hunting. It is thought that, in the ensuing dispute over the deer, Constantine was so touched by the divine Spirit evident within this man that he decided to commit his life and kingdom to the God of Petroc.

Stories abound of Petroc performing miracles and healings, and banishing monsters and dragons. One story tells of a monstrous serpent in Cornwall, a terrible heritage left by the recently dead king, who had been in the habit of throwing liars and thieves into a snake-filled pit, to be eaten alive. This form of execution was stopped when the king died, but the serpents were left in the pit. They became hungry now they were not being fed criminals, and so began to eat each another. Those that ate grew bigger and bigger, until finally only one remained, now of a monstrous size. This serpent escaped the pit and sought out other food. It began to eat the local livestock and people.

Petroc saw that his years of study, penance and quiet contemplation were all for this—that he might stand with God and face this serpent which terrorised the land.

Petroc set out for the beast's lair to free the land by removing the terrible serpent. Samson and Wethinoc joined him on the way and the three of them together, with great boldness and haste, came to where the serpent lived, the bones of the serpent's victims strewn about the place. They spoke no word, but simply stood before the entrance. The presence of these three men who embodied the holiness of God was the only thing needed. The giant serpent at first resisted, yet the heavy presence of holiness in them tore the creature from its lair. Petroc bound it with his own clothing and the three saints commanded the monster to leave Cornwall's shores and be gone into the sea. Like the swine at the command of Jesus, the serpent submitted and swam away, and was never seen in that land again.

After 30 years, legend says, Petroc went on the pilgrimage to Rome by way of Brittany. The place of his death was reputedly at a house belonging to a family named Rovel. The house is thought to be a farm now called Treravel, near Little Petherick—Little Petroc.

Meditation

Spend a few moments simply resting. Breathe gently and slowly. Become aware of the constant presence of God which envelops you and permeates you.

Petroc was a man of journey and of solitude. He spent time alone with God and travelling for him, performing miraculous signs and wonders. In this time he would have cultivated the presence of God within himself, and this was of such influence that King Constantine decided to dedicate himself and his entire kingdom to the God of Petroc.

In what way does God work through you? What do you do in order to create opportunities for God to work through you to influence others?

Spend time with God now, dwelling upon these questions.

Scripture

One day Elisha went to the town of Shunem. A wealthy woman lived there, and she urged him to come to her home for a meal. After that, whenever he passed that way, he would stop there for something to eat.

She said to her husband, 'I am sure this man who stops in from time to time is a holy man of God. Let's build a small room for him on the roof and furnish it with a bed, a table, a chair, and a lamp. Then he will have a place to stay whenever he comes by.'

One day Elisha returned to Shunem, and he went up to this upper room to rest. He said to his servant Gehazi, 'Tell the woman from Shunem I want to speak to her.' When she appeared, Elisha said to Gehazi, 'Tell her, "We appreciate the kind concern you have shown us. What can we do for you? Can we put in a good word for you to the king or to the commander of the army?"'

'No,' she replied, 'my family takes good care of me.'

Later Elisha asked Gehazi, 'What can we do for her?'

Gehazi replied, 'She doesn't have a son, and her husband is an old man.'

'Call her back again,' Elisha told him. When the woman returned, Elisha said to her as she stood in the doorway, 'Next year at this time you will be holding a son in your arms!'

'No, my lord!' she cried. 'O man of God, don't deceive me and get my hopes up like that.'

But sure enough, the woman soon became pregnant. And at that time the following year she had a son, just as Elisha had said.
2 KINGS 4:8–17 (NLT)

Blessing

May you be willing to allow God to work within you.
May you be an example to others of God's love for the world.
May you stand strong for God, and may God work through you to
change others' hearts.

36
Piran

FEAST DAY: 5 March (d.480)

Piran was an Irishman who travelled to Cornwall. Legend says that he travelled on a floating millstone. Local heathens in Ireland had tied him to it and thrown him into the sea as a form of execution, but the millstone floated on the ocean surface and took Piran to Cornwall.

While he was in Cornwall his hearthstone began to 'leak' tin, which poured out over the flat black stone in the shape of a cross. This image, a black background with a white cross, has become the design of the Cornish national flag.

Piran may be the same person as the Irish Saint Ciarán of Saigi, as the sounds of the letters P and K were sometimes alternated in Brittonic and Goidelic languages. The writer of the 14th-century *Life of Saint Piran* believed this to be the case, and so his writing is a copy of an earlier Irish *Life* of Saint Ciarán. If it is true that Piran and Ciaran were one and the same person, then Piran of Cornwall was one of the twelve apostles of Ireland who trained under Finnian at Clonard.

Before he was conceived, Piran's mother had a dream that a star fell into her mouth. She related this dream to the druids, who were knowledgeable about such things, and they told her that she would bear a son whose fame and virtues would be known as far as the world's end.[77] This came true in the life and mission of Piran.

Meditation

Spend a few moments simply resting. Breathe gently and slowly. Become aware of the constant presence of God which envelops you and permeates you.

Piran saw miraculous things happen to him, through him and around him, such as the floating millstone and the stone leaking tin in the shape of a cross. God spoke to his mother before he was born through a vision and showed her that he would be great.

In what way do you see miraculous things happening around you? Do you only class 'big things' as miracles? Are the miracles of God sometimes subtle? How might you become more aware of the miracles that God performs to you, through you and around you?

Spend time with God now, dwelling upon these questions.

Scripture

Now may the God of hope fill you with all joy and peace in believing, that you may abound in hope, in the power of the Holy Spirit. I myself am also persuaded about you, my brothers, that you yourselves are full of goodness, filled with all knowledge, able also to admonish others. But I write the more boldly to you in part, as reminding you, because of the grace that was given to me by God, that I should be a servant of Christ Jesus to the Gentiles, serving as a priest of the Good News of God, that the offering up of the Gentiles might be made acceptable, sanctified by the Holy Spirit. I have therefore my boasting in Christ Jesus in things pertaining to God. For I will not dare to speak of any things except those which Christ worked through me, for the obedience of the Gentiles, by word and deed, in the power of signs and wonders, in the power of God's Spirit; so that from Jerusalem, and around as far as to Illyricum, I have fully preached the Good

News of Christ; yes, making it my aim to preach the Good News, not where Christ was already named, that I might not build on another's foundation

ROMANS 15:13–20

Blessing

May you know the power of God at work within you.
May you see the miraculous happening around you.
May you be willing to allow God to work through you in whatever
  way he wills.

37

Samson

FEAST DAY: 28 July (d.565)

The *Life* written of this Welsh saint is said to be the most historically accurate and least hagiographic of all the records of the Celtic saints, but this doesn't stop the life of Samson being filled with amazing miracles of healing and supernatural encounters.

Samson was brought up as a pagan or druid and was known to possess power in 'the arts'—dark spiritual power. He soon turned his back on this way of life, became filled with the Spirit of God and taught and lived the life of Christ. He trained under the guidance of Illtyd alongside both David and Gildas. When he was consecrated in the church by Illtyd, he had a spiritual visitation: a dove came and floated above him as a sign of the power of God resting upon him.

On one occasion, a man needed healing and none of the other monks, including Illtyd, were having any success. Samson asked if he could have a turn, as he could use the power of his Father. Knowing Samson's upbringing, Illtyd mistakenly thought that Samson wanted to use the pagan druidic magic of his earthly father, but Samson assured him that he meant his heavenly Father. Illtyd allowed him to try, and the man was healed.

On another occasion, after Samson had raised a child from the dead, bringing a tribe to worship Christ instead of an idol, the chief of the tribe saw that there was great supernatural power in Samson and asked him to confront a 'poisonous and very vicious serpent'.[78] The serpent lived in a cave between two villages and was destroying them both. Samson told the chief to lead him to the cave, which he did. Samson, with God beside him, boldly entered the cave alone.

> The serpent, however, as soon as it saw [Samson], trembled exceedingly and was disposed to turn itself and bite its tail with passion; but he, quickly seizing the linen girdle that was around him, without more ado, slipped it on its neck, and dragging the beast near to him, flung it from a certain height and charged it in the name of Jesus not to live any longer.[79]

Meditation

Spend a few moments simply resting. Breathe gently and slowly. Become aware of the constant presence of God which envelops you and permeates you.

In the life of Samson we see the turning of one who was pagan into one filled with the Spirit and power of God. Unlike Kevin of Glendalough, who tamed a beast and lived with it, Samson saw that he needed to get rid of his beast in the name of Jesus Christ. There are times when we need to tame, and times when we must clean out.

Is there any area of your inner self that needs to be cleansed in the name of Jesus Christ? Are there any 'serpents' which need the hand of God to get rid of them? (You might want to talk and pray with someone else about this.)

Spend time with God now, dwelling upon these questions.

Scripture

> They came to the other side of the sea, into the country of the Gadarenes. When he had come out of the boat, immediately a

man with an unclean spirit met him out of the tombs. He lived in the tombs. Nobody could bind him any more, not even with chains, because he had been often bound with fetters and chains, and the chains had been torn apart by him, and the fetters broken in pieces. Nobody had the strength to tame him. Always, night and day, in the tombs and in the mountains, he was crying out, and cutting himself with stones. When he saw Jesus from afar, he ran and bowed down to him, and crying out with a loud voice, he said, 'What have I to do with you, Jesus, you Son of the Most High God? I adjure you by God, don't torment me.' For he said to him, 'Come out of the man, you unclean spirit!'

He asked him, 'What is your name?'

He said to him, 'My name is Legion, for we are many.' He begged him much that he would not send them away out of the country. Now on the mountainside there was a great herd of pigs feeding. All the demons begged him, saying, 'Send us into the pigs, that we may enter into them.'

At once Jesus gave them permission. The unclean spirits came out and entered into the pigs. The herd of about two thousand rushed down the steep bank into the sea, and they were drowned in the sea. Those who fed them fled, and told it in the city and in the country.

The people came to see what it was that had happened. They came to Jesus, and saw him who had been possessed by demons sitting, clothed, and in his right mind, even him who had the legion; and they were afraid. Those who saw it declared to them what happened to him who was possessed by demons, and about the pigs.

MARK 5:1–16

Blessing

May you be willing to be led from old ways into new ways.
May you be filled with the power of the Holy Spirit to work miracles,
both large and small.
May you know the freedom of Christ when the influence of spiritual
darkness is cleansed from your inner being.
May you be willing, like Samson, to be sent out into the 'harvest field'
to do God's will and live a life of authenticity for God.

38
Teilo

FEAST DAY: 9 February (d.560)

Teilo was born in Wales and grew to become an influential, though largely forgotten saint. He was a contemporary of David and Samson. Teilo travelled with David on pilgrimage to Jerusalem, where they were both, along with others, consecrated as bishops. They were also together when David planted the community in the place that is now St David's on the west coast of Wales.

Teilo travelled throughout Wales himself, preaching and planting communities of God, but then an outbreak of yellow fever drove him and his community out of Wales. They moved to Cornwall for a time, and finally to Dol in Brittany, where Teilo stayed and ministered for seven years with Samson. They are said to have planted three miles of fruit trees there.

Teilo and his followers returned from Brittany to Llandeilo Fawr. After the death of David, Teilo became revered as one of the most holy men in Wales. He was also at Llandaff. Dyfrig founded a community close to the River Taff, where Llandaff cathedral now stands, and was succeeded as leader of the community by Teilo. Nothing remains of the original church, but a Celtic cross that stood nearby can still be seen near the door of the chapter house. There is also a large Celtic cross in the grounds of Llandaff Cathedral with a ninth-century date on it.

Teilo died at the abbey of Llandeilo Fawr, but his skull is housed in a vault at Llandaff Cathedral. Much folklore surrounds the history of Teilo's skull.

Meditation

Spend a few moments simply resting. Breathe gently and slowly. Become aware of the constant presence of God which envelops you and permeates you.

At one time, Teilo was revered as one of the most holy men in Wales. He planted churches (and fruit trees), travelled and learned with well-known saints, yet today he is almost unknown.

In what way do you want to be remembered? Do you want your name to be known, or are you content simply to do what God calls you to do, even if your name is forgotten? What recognition do you desire for what you do?

Spend time with God now, dwelling upon these questions.

Scripture

I commend to you Phoebe, our sister, who is a servant of the assembly that is at Cenchreae, that you receive her in the Lord, in a way worthy of the saints, and that you assist her in whatever matter she may need from you, for she herself also has been a helper of many, and of my own self.

Greet Prisca and Aquila, my fellow workers in Christ Jesus, who for my life, laid down their own necks; to whom not only I give thanks, but also all the assemblies of the Gentiles. Greet the assembly that is in their house. Greet Epaenetus, my beloved, who is the first fruits of Achaia to Christ. Greet Mary, who laboured much for us. Greet Andronicus and Junia, my relatives and my fellow prisoners, who are notable among the apostles, who were also in Christ before me. Greet Amplias, my beloved in the Lord. Greet Urbanus, our fellow worker in Christ, and Stachys, my beloved. Greet Apelles, the approved in Christ. Greet those who are of the household of Aristobulus. Greet Herodion, my kinsman. Greet them of the household of Narcissus, who are in the Lord. Greet Tryphaena and Tryphosa, who labour in the Lord. Greet Persis, the beloved, who laboured much in the Lord. Greet Rufus, the chosen in the Lord, and his mother and mine. Greet Asyncritus, Phlegon, Hermes, Patrobas, Hermas, and the brothers who are with them. Greet Philologus and Julia, Nereus and his sister, and Olympas, and all the saints who are with them. Greet one another with a holy kiss. The assemblies of Christ greet you…

Timothy, my fellow worker, greets you, as do Lucius, Jason, and Sosipater, my relatives. I, Tertius, who write the letter, greet you in the Lord. Gaius, my host and host of the whole assembly, greets you. Erastus, the treasurer of the city, greets you, as does Quartus, the brother. The grace of our Lord Jesus Christ be with you all! Amen.

ROMANS 16:1–16, 21–24

Blessing

May you follow God's direction without faltering.
May you be great in all you do.
May you be content to do these things with no recognition or
  remembrance of your name.

39
Tysilio

FEAST DAY: 8 November (d.640)

Prince Tysilio was the younger son of King Brychwel Ysgithrog, who, as a prince himself, had discovered Melangell in a valley within his land. The influence of Melangell had obviously remained with Brychwel Ysgithrog and within his kingdom, and had been passed on to his children. As a young child, Tysilio, with his friends and siblings, may have even visited Melangell and been witness to the 'miracles and various other signs [which were not] lacking for those who called upon her help'.[80]

Tysilio grew up in turbulent times of kingdom wars, and fled his father's court to become a monk. He spent some time travelling around Wales, teaching and preaching and planting churches, and then became a hermit for some time on Ynys Tysilio in the Menai Straits. He also spent seven years teaching and preaching on Ynys Mon (Anglesey) and planting churches there. The most famous of Tysilio's churches is on Ynys Mon and is one of the locations mentioned in the longest place name in Britain: Llanfairpwllgwyngyllgogerychwyrndrobwll*llantysilio*gogogoch. This translates roughly as 'Church of Mary in the Hollow of the White Hazel near a Rapid Whirlpool and the Church of Tysilio near the Red Cave'.

After the death of Tysilio's elder brother, who had inherited the throne from their father, his sister-in-law, Queen Gwenwynwyn, wanted to marry Tysilio and have him as king. When he objected to both proposals, his monastery came under the scorn of the queen and suffered persecution from her and her political influence. Eventually, he decided to move to Brittany with a small band of followers. They crossed the Channel and travelled to Saint-Suliac, where Tysilio established another monastery.

Tysilio died in the monastery in Saint-Suliac and was buried there.

Meditation

Spend a few moments simply resting. Breathe gently and slowly. Become aware of the constant presence of God which envelops you and permeates you.

Tysilio fled the royal life in which he had grown up, and lived a holy life dedicated to God and his calling. Later, he was summoned back to his old lifestyle and could easily have returned to it, this time as king. Perhaps he could have had a large influence, like Oswald in Northumbria. But Tysilio was not tempted, as he knew God was not calling him to it.

What have you given up for God? In what ways are you tempted to drift back into that way of life, or to take those things up again? How might you be better able to overcome any such suggestions, either from external or internal forces?

Spend time with God now, dwelling upon these questions.

Scripture

On that day Jesus went out of the house, and sat by the seaside. Great multitudes gathered to him, so that he entered into a boat, and sat, and all the multitude stood on the beach. He spoke to them many things in parables, saying, 'Behold, a farmer went out to sow. As he sowed, some seeds fell by the roadside, and the birds came and devoured them. Others fell on rocky ground, where they didn't have much soil, and immediately they sprang up, because they had no depth of earth. When the sun had risen, they were scorched. Because they had no root, they withered away. Others fell among thorns. The thorns grew up and choked them. Others fell on good soil, and yielded fruit: some one hundred times as much, some sixty, and some thirty. He who has ears to hear, let him hear.'...

'Hear, then, the parable of the farmer. When anyone hears the word of the Kingdom, and doesn't understand it, the evil one comes, and snatches away that which has been sown in his heart. This is what was sown by the roadside. What was sown on the rocky places, this is he who hears the word, and immediately with joy receives it; yet he has no root in himself, but endures for a while. When oppression or persecution arises because of the word, immediately he stumbles. What was sown among the thorns, this is he who hears the word, but the cares of this age and the deceitfulness of riches choke the word, and he becomes unfruitful. What was sown on the good ground, this is he who hears the word, and understands it, who most certainly bears fruit, and produces, some one hundred times as much, some sixty, and some thirty.'

MATTHEW 13:1-9, 18-23

Blessing

May you know the life that God is calling you from and to.
May you be willing to give up everything that God asks you to.
May you have the strength to remain in God's will, even if the things that God has called you away from are offered back to you.

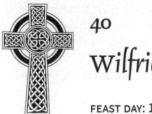

40
Wilfrid

FEAST DAY: 12 October (d.709)

Wilfrid was trained on Lindisfarne, where, as an intellectual young man, he quickly learned the Psalms and other books. After some years on Lindisfarne, Wilfrid grew discontented with the way of life taught there and resolved to travel to Rome, where he believed a more academic approach to the faith could be found. In Rome, Wilfrid grew in his learning and knowledge and took the Roman tonsure. On his return to Britain, he took charge of the monastic centre in Ripon, which had originally been given to the Celtic church. It had housed Cuthbert at one time, but, when the local king took on the Roman way of Christianity, the Celts in Ripon refused to change their way of life and had to leave the place.

Because of his renowned and well-respected intellect, Wilfrid was given the task, at the Synod of Whitby, of arguing the case for the Roman side. He was perhaps asked to do this as he also had inside knowledge of the Celtic way of life and dating of Easter from his training on Lindisfarne.

Wilfrid later became the bishop of York. However, Bede tells us this:

> There arose a dissention between King Ecgfrith and the most reverend bishop Wilfrid with the result that the bishop was driven from his see, while two bishops were put in his place to rule over the Northumbrian race... When Wilfrid had been expelled from his see he spent a long time travelling in many lands, going to Rome and afterwards returning to Britain. Though he could not be received back into his own native land and diocese... he turned to the kingdom of the South Saxons.[81]

Later, being allowed to return to the north under the next king, Aldfrith, Wilfrid had another altercation and was driven out of his see for the second time. He travelled to Rome to plead his case, where the Pope and the council found that not all the charges against him were true. On his journey home, Wilfrid became severely unwell but eventually recovered. When he eventually returned to the north of England, King Aldfrith did not receive him back, but this situation was not to last as the king died soon after Wilfrid's return. The next new king, Osred, did allow Wilfrid back home, after a heated meeting where the decision was made. Wilfrid lived there for another four years, until he died. 'He died in his own monastery in the district of Oundle, while Abbot Cuthbald was ruling over it; he was carried by the brothers to his first monastery at Ripon and buried [there].'[82]

Meditation

Spend a few moments simply resting. Breathe gently and slowly. Become aware of the constant presence of God which envelops you and permeates you.

Wilfrid was a highly intellectual man and grew famous for the extent of his knowledge. For many who love and study Celtic Christianity today, the life of Wilfrid is a stark reminder of the draw of greed and power, and the difference between being steadfast in your beliefs and being arrogant and stubborn.

How do you understand the difference between standing firm for what you believe and being arrogant and stubborn? Have you ever exhibited both characteristics? How might you cultivate the steadfastness without becoming stubborn?

Spend time with God now, dwelling upon these questions.

Scripture

Show me your ways, Yahweh.
   Teach me your paths.
Guide me in your truth, and teach me,
   For you are the God of my salvation,
   I wait for you all day long.
Yahweh, remember your tender mercies and your loving kindness,
   for they are from old times.
Don't remember the sins of my youth, nor my transgressions.
   Remember me according to your loving kindness,
   for your goodness' sake, Yahweh.
Good and upright is Yahweh,
   therefore he will instruct sinners in the way.
He will guide the humble in justice.
   He will teach the humble his way.
All the paths of Yahweh are loving kindness and truth
   to such as keep his covenant and his testimonies.
For your name's sake, Yahweh,
   pardon my iniquity, for it is great.
What man is he who fears Yahweh?
   He shall instruct him in the way that he shall choose.
His soul shall dwell at ease.
   His offspring shall inherit the land.
The friendship of Yahweh is with those who fear him.
   He will show them his covenant.

PSALM 25:4–14

Blessing

May you always be strong in your faith.
May you stand firm in your call and in what you believe.
May you also know the difference between steadfastness and
   stubbornness.

The 40 saints

IN ORDER OF THEIR FEAST DAYS

Bibliography

Anam Chara Books, *The Celtic Study Bible* (Anam Chara, 2016).

Christopher Bamford, *The Voice of the Eagle: The heart of Celtic Christianity—John Scotus Eriugena's homily on the prologue to the Gospel of John* (Lindisfarne, 2000).

Bede, *The Ecclesiastical History of the English People* (Oxford University Press, 1999).

Bede, *Life of St Cuthbert*, in Bertram Colgrave (trans.), *Two Lives of Saint Cuthbert* (Christ the King Library, undated).

Robert Boenig, *Anglo-Saxon Spirituality: Selected writings* (Paulist Press, 2000).

Julius Caesar, *The Gallic Wars and other writings* (Random House, 1969).

Bertram Colgrave (trans.), *Two Lives of Saint Cuthbert* (Christ the King Library, undated).

Kevin Crossley-Holland, *The Anglo-Saxon World: An anthology* (Oxford University Press, 2009).

Oliver Davies, *Celtic Spirituality* (Paulist Press, 1999).

Gildas, *On the Ruin of Britain* (Serenity, 2009).

Bob Hartman, *Early Saints of God* (Augsburg, 1998).

Eleanor Hull, *Early Christian Ireland* (Kindle edition).

Wentworth Huyshe, *The Life of Saint Columba by Adamnan* (George Routledge & Sons, 1939).

Kenneth McIntosh, *Water from an Ancient Well* (Anam Chara, 2011).

Thomas Merton, *New Seeds of Contemplation* (Shambhala, 2003).

Maurice O'Connor, *Life of Saint Kieran of Saighir* (Kindle edition).

Noel Dermot O'Donoghue, *Aristocracy of the Soul: Patrick of Ireland* (DLT, 1987).

Uinseann ÓMaidin, *The Celtic Monk* (Cistercian Publications, 1996).

Tim Severin, *The Brendan Voyage* (Hutchinson, 1978).

Ray Simpson, *A Guide for Soul Friends: The art of the spiritual companion* (Kevin Mayhew, 2008).

Ray Simpson, *Celtic Daily Light* (Kevin Mayhew, 2003).

Ray Simpson, *Hilda of Whitby: A spirituality for now* (BRF, 2014).

Ray Simpson, *St Aidan's Way of Mission* (BRF, 2016).

Ray Simpson, *Saints of the Isles* (Kevin Mayhew, 2003).

Thomas Taylor, *The Life of Samson of Dol* (Kessinger Legacy Reprints, 1925).

J.R.R. Tolkien, *Angles and Britons* (University of Wales Press, 1963).

Kate Tristram, *Columbanus: The earliest voice of Christian Ireland* (Columba Press, 2010).

Myra L. Uhlfelder, *Periphyseon: On the division of nature by John the Scot* (Wipf and Stock, undated).

Notes

1 J.R.R Tolkien, *Angles and Britons* (University of Wales Press, 1963), p. 29.
2 Julius Caesar, *The Gallic Wars and other writings* (Random House, 1969), p. 1 (italics mine).
3 Oliver Davies, *Celtic Spirituality* (Paulist Press, 1999), p. 11.
4 Thomas O'Loughlin, *Celtic Theology* (Continuum, 2003), p. 2.
5 For a fuller understanding of this, see Kenneth McIntosh, *Water from an Ancient Well* (Anam Chara, 2011), ch. 4, 'The crux of life: the meaning of the cross'.
6 From Kevin Crossley-Holland (ed., trans.), *The Anglo-Saxon World* (Boydell Press, 2004).
7 Bede, *The Ecclesiastical History of the English People* (Oxford University Press, 1999), Book 5, ch. 15.
8 Bede, *Ecclesiastical History*, Book 5, chs 16 and 17.
9 Eleanor Hull, *Early Christian Ireland* (Kindle edition).
10 Bede, *Ecclesiastical History*, Book 5, ch. 15.
11 Bede, *Ecclesiastical History*, Book 5, ch. 15.
12 Bede, *Ecclesiastical History*, Book 4, ch. 25.
13 Bede, *Ecclesiastical History*, Book 4, ch. 25.
14 Bede, *Ecclesiastical History*, Book 4, ch. 25.
15 Both quotations in this paragraph: Bede, *Ecclesiastical History*, Book 3, ch. 5.
16 Bede, *Ecclesiastical History*, Book 3, ch. 25.
17 Bede, *Ecclesiastical History*, Book 3, ch. 17.
18 See Ray Simpson, *A Guide for Soul Friends: The art of the spiritual companion* (Kevin Mayhew, 2008) and Edward Sellner, *The Celtic Soul Friend: A trusted guide for today* (Ave Maria Press, 2002).
19 Bede, *Ecclesiastical History*, Book 4, ch. 27.
20 See 'The voyage of Brendan' in Oliver Davies, *Celtic Spirituality* (Paulist Press, 1999), p. 156.
21 Davies, *Celtic Spirituality*, p. 158.
22 Davies, *Celtic Spirituality*, p. 182.
23 Davies, *Celtic Spirituality*, p. 189.
24 Davies, *Celtic Spirituality*, p. 174.
25 Davies, *Celtic Spirituality*, p. 175.
26 See Tim Severin, *The Brendan Voyage* (Hutchinson, 1978).

27 See Bob Hartman, *Early Saints of God* (Augsburg, 1998) and 'The life of St Brigit the Virgin by Cognitosus' in Davies, *Celtic Spirituality*.
28 See www.youtube.com/watch?v=bq0ci42PnLc for a video on 'How to make a Brigid's cross from rushes'.
29 Bede, *Ecclesiastical History*, Book 4, ch. 24.
30 A poem by Tom Stamp found in *Collected Whitby Poems* (copyright ownership currently unknown).
31 Bede, *Ecclesiastical History*, Book 3, ch. 23.
32 Bede, *Ecclesiastical History*, Book 3, ch. 25.
33 Bede, *Ecclesiastical History*, Book 3, ch. 23.
34 See Hull, *Early Christian Ireland*, ch. 2.
35 Bede, *Ecclesiastical History*, Book 3, ch. 26.
36 Bede, *Ecclesiastical History*, Book 3, ch. 25.
37 Bede, *Ecclesiastical History*, Book 3, ch. 26.
38 Dál Riata (also Dalriada or Dalriata) was an Irish kingdom which included parts of western Scotland and north-eastern Ulster in Ireland. In the late sixth to early seventh century it encompassed roughly what is now Argyll and Lochaber in Scotland and County Antrim in Ulster.
39 Wentworth Huyshe, *The Life of Saint Columba by Adamnan* (George Routledge & Sons, 1939), Book 3, ch. 15.
40 Thomas Merton, *New Seeds of Contemplation* (Shambhala, 2003), p. 270.
41 Kate Tristram, *Columbanus: The earliest voice of Christian Ireland* (Columba Press, 2010), p. 16.
42 For a fuller understanding of this, see McIntosh, *Water from an Ancient Well*, ch. 6, 'Green martyrs—spiritual fitness'. For further reading, see Richard Foster, *Celebration of Discipline* (Hodder and Stoughton, 2008).
43 Uinseann ÓMaidin, *The Celtic Monk* (Cistercian Publications, 1996), 'The Rule of Comgall', p. 31.
44 ÓMaidin, *The Celtic Monk*, p. 35.
45 ÓMaidin, *The Celtic Monk*, p. 32.
46 Bede's prose *Life of St Cuthbert*, ch. 13.
47 Bede, *Life of St Cuthbert*, ch. 13.
48 Rhigyfarch, 'The Life of St David' in Davies, *Celtic Spirituality*, pp. 197–98.
49 Found in *The Book of Kilkenny*.
50 Gildas, *On the Ruin of Britain* (Serenity, 2009), 'The History', section 8.
51 Bede, *Ecclesiastical History*, Book 4, ch. 29.
52 Bede, *Ecclesiastical History*, Book 4, ch. 29.

53   Bede, *Ecclesiastical History*, Book 4, ch. 29.

54   Bede, *Ecclesiastical History*, Book 4, ch. 29.

55   For more information about soul friendship, see Ray Simpson, *A Guide for Soul Friends*.

56   Bede, *Ecclesiastical History*, Book 4, ch. 23.

57   Taken from Ray Simpson, *Hilda of Whitby: A spirituality for now* (BRF, 2014).

58   Davies, *Celtic Spirituality*, p. 58.

59   John Scotus Eriugena, *Periphyseon: On the division of nature*, Book 1, ch. 8, in Myra L. Uhlfelder, *Periphyseon: On the division of nature by John the Scot* (Wipf and Stock, undated).

60   Christopher Bamford (trans.), *The Voice of the Eagle: The heart of Celtic Christianity: John Scotus Eriugena's Homily on the prologue to the Gospel of St John* (Lindisfarne Books, 2000), p. 86.

61   *Periphyseon*, Book 1, ch. 72.

62   Huyshe, *The Life of Saint Columba by Adamnan*, p. 24.

63   Huyshe, *The Life of Saint Columba by Adamnan*, p. 68.

64   Huyshe, *The Life of Saint Columba by Adamnan*, p. xxxiii.

65   Davies, *Celtic Spirituality*, p. 221.

66   Davies, *Celtic Spirituality*, p. 222.

67   Davies, *Celtic Spirituality*, p. 222.

68   Bede, *Ecclesiastical History*, Book 3, ch. 9.

69   Bede, *Ecclesiastical History*, Book 3, ch. 5.

70   Bede, *Ecclesiastical History*, Book 3, ch. 6.

71   Bede, *Ecclesiastical History*, Book 3, ch. 7.

72   *The Confession of Patrick*, C.H.H. Wright (trans.) from Noel D. O'Donoghue, *Aristocracy of the Soul: Patrick of Ireland* (DLT, 1987), p. 101.

73   Davies, *Celtic Spirituality*, p. 21.

74   James P. Mackey, *An Introduction to Celtic Christianity* (T&T Clark, 1995), pp. 389–90.

75   See the study notes on Matthew 7 in *The Celtic Study Bible* (Anam Chara). This is partially published, as an ebook, 2016.

76   Davies, *Celtic Spirituality*, p. 56.

77   Maurice O'Connor, *Life of Saint Kieran of Saighir* (Kindle edition).

78   Thomas Taylor, *The Life of Samson of Dol* (Kessinger Legacy Reprints, 1925), ch. 50.

79   Taylor, *The Life of Samson of Dol*, ch. 50.

80   Davies, *Celtic Spirituality*, p. 222.

81   Bede, *Ecclesiastical History*, Book 4, chs 12 and 13.

82   Bede, *Ecclesiastical History*, Book 5, ch. 19.